George H. (George Herman) Ellwanger

Meditations on Gout

With a Consideration of its Cure through the use of Wine

George H. (George Herman) Ellwanger

Meditations on Gout
With a Consideration of its Cure through the use of Wine

ISBN/EAN: 9783337211585

Printed in Europe, USA, Canada, Australia, Japan

Cover: Foto ©Andreas Hilbeck / pixelio.de

More available books at **www.hansebooks.com**

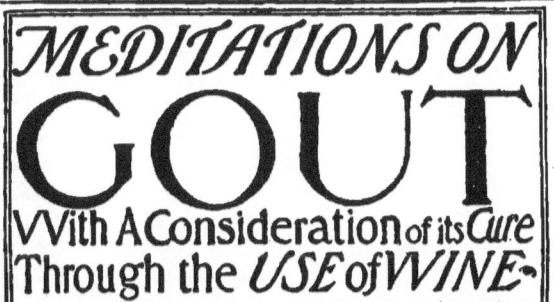

MEDITATIONS ON
GOUT

With A Consideration of its Cure
Through the USE of WINE

BY

George H. Ellwanger. MA

Author of "The Story of MY HOUSE
"IDYLLISTS of the COUNTRY SIDE"
ETC·ETC

With a FRONTISPIECE & DECORATION by
George Wharton Edwards

NEW YORK DODD·MEAD & COMPANY

MEDITATIONS ON GOUT

Like as a wily Foxe, that having spide,
Where on a sunnie banke the Lambes doo play,
Full closely creeping by the hinder side,
Lyes in ambushment of his hopèd pray.

SPENSER: *The Fate of the Butterfly.*

PREMONSTRATION

Read many such, and then ask what is to be done.
ROBERT BURTON, *The Anatomy of Melancholy.*

 *T already entereth into the ken of the Physician, and the General Reader may be made to perceive in like degree that all formulæ how subtile soever for the assuagement and* ordering of Gout *are Not Absolute. It is not within the power of The Author, therefore (nor would it comport with the exact scope of his Theme), to propound,* even through the use of Wine, *a general and unconditional* Cure : *such depending not only on the idiosyncrasies of the Malady, but upon the divers stomachic fantasies, rheums, defluxions, humours, crudities, and assimilative vagaries of the Individual, as*
will

vii

Premonstration

will be duly set forth in the following chapters.
Forasmuch as no two leaves are precisely alike,
nay, no two grains of sand resemble each other,
so likewise no two Gouts *are of identical habit*
and complexion.

And of those who affirm that Wine *engender-*
eth it, how many be there who rightly compre-
hend the proper governing and Virtues of Wines,
how wisely to choose and fitly to make use of
them, —

Hor. lib. 1,
Od. 18, 3.
Siccis omnia nam dura deus proposuit, neque
Mordaces aliter diffugiunt sollicitudines, —

To the lips of the dry does the godhead taint all with a taste
of the sour,
And only by wine are the troubles gnawing into the bosom
dispersed, —

since in those countries where it is most cus-
tomarily employed, do we not find the disease to
be both the less frequent and the more amenable ?
For be it known that Physicke *(from the time*
of Hippocrates to the Present) hath but served
to foster and sharpen the Malady, rather than
to

Premonstration

to mend it. Else wherefore with such glut of Physicians and store of Medicine, doth the gird of Gout *still wherret and harass in such exceeding great degree? Its girdings pursue us upon our journeys and in our rooms, even into lonely places and business-marts.* Nor doe hollow rocks, nor wearing of haire-shirts, nor continuall fastings rid us from them. *And that it is a sickness brought about by feasting and intemperance, do we not see to the contrary when Philosophers, Physicians, Counselors, Ambassadors, Grammar-School Masters, aye, Popes, Priests, Friars, and many of the Ecclesiastical profession are grievously smitten by it?*

Yet is it that of those who in books and discourses have touched upon the Malady, Sydenham hath shown himself most worthy of his Art (yea, chief-craftsman of such craft), whereby the use of Wine *is sanctioned or condemned, as the writer is governed by prejudice or melted by sympathy. And if not in words, at least by their actions, say they for the most part with Dr.*
Purgon:

Montaigne. Of Solitarinesse.

Premonstration

Molière, Le
Malade
Imaginaire. *Purgon :* J'ai à vous dire que je vous abandonne
à votre mauvaise constitution, à l'intempérie de
vos entrailles, à la corruption de votre sang, à
l'âcreté de votre bile, & à la féculence de vos
humeurs. (I abandon you to your miserable
constitution, to the inclemency of your vitals,
to the corruption of your blood, to the acrid-
ness of your bile, & to the leaven of your
humours.)

*Lo, the burden of these their Doctrines and
the inconstancies of their Opinions, with which
they disport like unto a juggler with his blades.
Some have avouched that Meats do provoke it,
others that Meats be beneficial. Some have declared that all manner of* Beers *lead there-
unto, others will have breadstuffs to be hurtful,
while some do commend them; some hold sal-
lets, asparagus, tomatoes, tubers, scarlet-run-
ners, and other such like to be poisonous;
others that all Fruit engendereth vapours and
humours; others that much Sleep is baneful;
some affirm the Hermodactyl hath some sullen,
churlish*

Premonstration

churlish conditions with it : others that of all
herbs it alone hath power to soothe.

   Saith one, strawberries are to be shunned;
saith another, they should be chosen; and the
third, they are good when moderately enjoyed.
The one affirmeth it to be beholden to Bacchus :
the other to Ceres, *and still another to* Venus.
No two hold to the same belief, and within their
ranks is there ever wrangling and contention.
The words of the wise are as goads, and as nails Eccles. xii. 12.
fastened by the masters of assemblies. *Verily,*
use they their calling to harrow and perplex;
and proffer a cure but to effect a temporary
hold-all, which profiteth chiefly themselves. The
Chirurgeon's knife, likewise, and his love of
operating, is he not fain to employ it on the
smallest pretext; and is it not oft in these latter
days the bent and jouissance of the specialist to
render woman unwomanly ?

> 'T is the Chirurgeon's praise and height of art,   Herrick,
> Not to cut off, but cure the vicious part.   Hesperides.

To the same purpose might the opinion of an
ancient Gallic philosopher be adjoined : The

Arts

Premonstration

Montaigne, Of Experience. Arts that promise to keepe our body and minde in good health promise much unto us; but therewith there is none performeth lesse what they promise.

And whereas it may be perceived in the reading of these Meditations how beneficent Wine *may prove in the treatment of the Evil, yet must it be manifest in like manner what* Artifice *it requireth to prescribe the exact sort that will meet the individual Case. This the Patient, or leastwise some wittly-wary Medical Mentor needs must choose, elect, and adjudge for himself from the amass of species, varieties, and vintages : at the hazard of aggravating the dangers of the Disease withal, if the kind most effectual for a* Remedy *be at first unapprehended. For may we rarely attain to any good result without studious reflection, or stress of toil ; and with the sweet must ever be mingled the bitter : —*

Ovid, Metam. 7. Usque adeo nulla est sincera voluptas,
Sollicitumque aliquid lætis intervenit.

Where is the pleasure marred by no alloy ?
Some apprehension ever haunts our joy.

Our

Premonstration

Our troubles still pursue us : —

Scilicet interdum miscentur tristia lætis,
Nec populum toto pectore festa juvant.

Ovid,
Fasti, 2.

*Grief mingles with our mirth, when at its best,
And robs our feasts of some part of their ʒest!*

*See we not constantly how little understand-
ing prevaileth in the* election of Wines; *whether
they be white or red, mantling or still, sharp or
balsamic, tawney or deep-coloured, and long or
quick to the taste: whether they be well-com-
plexioned full pleasant Malmseys; fat Bastards
or Allicants; pale Sacks that have lain long;
Muskadine that is strong and of sweet scent;
nutty yellow Canaries; or Rhenish of* Elstertune
or of Barabant: *whether they be the* river, *or the*
mountain *grey sorts of Champaign, in colour
like unto a partridge's eye, and fashioned after
the manner of that most worthy monk, Perignon;
the wines* de Garde *near* Nuis *and* Chambertin *of
which Lewis the Fourteenth drank no other kind;
or Gascoine wines that be made in the Castles
about* Bourdeaux, *of which Château* Margouze *and*
O'Brion

xiii

Premonstration

O'Brion *possess the most ambrosial flavour. And of these last, whether they be fair-hued, ruby-bright, pleasant at the Nose, and smelling of the Rose or Violet, rather than those that be deep-hued as the Amethyst and savour of the soil; or such as have lost their colour as happeneth ofttimes to Burgundy and Claret wines, causing them to become mustulent and to drink faint. There be divers other sorts, in the choosing of which the Physician may have part for the guidance and governance of* Gout, *as seemeth best to his judgment and understanding: as those white Gascoine kinds, in colour like unto light Amber that are known as* Graves, Saint-Cross of the Mount, *and* Between Two Seas, *according to their district, whose properties are dry, cooling, and of a diuretic nature; aye, whose very fragrance is cool. For that which most profiteth one, is oft most cloysome to another; and* in nought do we observe so great disparity and so contrary effects as in Wines. *Some do cheer while others do grievously offend, in the same manner that ob-*

taineth

taineth with certain smells and odours. And moreover what comporteth at one time may prove hurtful at another, according to the season, and the Mood of the Malady.

Never are we alway of the same precise temper and fantasy, nor may we ever wisely hold to the self-same way. Neither may we truly learn what best befitteth us save by experience, and by the infixing of laws, each unto himself, for his proper profit and understanding. Age calleth for joys other than such as be meted out to Youth in his April's flower, and the march of Time doth alter the power of wonted things to allure, or to conduce to health and bodily wants. As we change in our reading of Books wherein those once fervently fondled do no longer fully satisfy and seize upon the mind, so our appetites waver and shift, and create new longings for the Body's need. And even as a weathervane doth vacillate and veer, and a stream turneth now to the right hand and now to the left, the while it glideth on its appointed course, so do advancing

Premonstration

vancing years cause us to deviate from those paths we have erstwhile followed :

Multa ferunt anni venientes commoda secum,
Multa recedentes adimunt.

Years, as they come, a host of blessings bring ;
A host of blessings, as they go, take wing.

Yet needs must balms for all diseases exist in the manifold products of the vegetable king-dom, do we but know how rightly to turn them to account, and seek we to avoid pernicious dainties which lead unto our ailments.

Verily, Hippocrates hath written much con-cerning his Art ; and Galen, Sydenham, Cullen, and Garrod have shown great ʒeal (albeit they have accomplished little) in search of a Wine *to assuage the pangs of the Malady.   But do as best beseemeth him, take what course he listeth, choose his simples as he may, the Physician often avail-eth little ; and peradventure fareth he best who boldly taketh the Evil in his own hands,* and thereof himself prescribeth The Cure.

G. H. E.

SCHÖNBERG, ROCHESTER, 1897.

SYLLABUS

THE MALADY

I

Meditations on Gout

THE MALADY

It is a kinde of maladie a man must fight withall.
MONTAIGNE.

OUT is so closely associated with the daily subsistence of civilised man, it is an evil of such frequent occurrence, accompanied by consequences of so serious a character, that a somewhat extended résumé of its history, ætiology, treatment, and aberrations may be of interest to the layman, by whom it is usually considered an infrequent malady,—the sequence of high-living and thorn in the rose of gastronomy, with many years of savoury dinners and fragrant vintages as its genesis and means of evolution. More or less allied to dyspepsia and kin to indigestion, it is,

3

nevertheless, a common affliction induced by widely varying causes, that since the days of the ancients has proved a weariness to the flesh and has yielded little to medication.

And while dyspepsia may well claim more than a passing word in discussing the question of good-cheer or in alluding to stomachic derangements, it is with wine and alcoholic fluids more especially that Gout is concerned and calls for specific consideration. For dyspepsia, except in rare instances, or where it exists in connection with other gastric disturbances of long standing or in themselves of a remarkably obdurate character, generally submits to treatment; whereas Gout, when once established, is for the most part beyond the means of permanent remedial control. Its prognosis presumably reads: *Unfavourable as regards complete and favourable recovery;* [1] or, *A permanent release from the disease is rarely to be hoped for.* [2] Even under the most favourable circumstances, it usually remains

[1] Prof. H. Senator, *Diseases of the Locomotive Apparatus.*
[2] Prof. Adolf Strümpell, *A Text Book of Medicine.*

4

like the vase and the attar-of-roses. Or so, at any rate, it has remained up to the close of the nineteenth century.

Of what is its nature, and of what is it constituted ? Is it generated from without, or is it fomented from within; is it caused by over-ingestion, or insufficient elimination, or both ; is it renal, hepatic, or neurotic in its character; or do all of these conditions play a part in the dyscrasia ? How far are involuntary causes responsible for its production, — causes independent of the individual, — and how far is man capable of palliating or averting the disease ? Thereon authorities disagree, and therein consist its idiosyncrasies. As no eye can detect the precise colour of the dragon-fly's wings as he darts in capricious flight and reflects the sunbeam from his irised mail, so no cunning of the analyst has been able to determine the true complexion of this protean disease, that has been handed down from times remote, and falls without warning upon the just and unjust still.

No other malady, not strictly organic, has

baffled medical science to so great an extent, the doctors themselves being frequently among its chosen victims, with whom it often flourishes under the more plebeian title of "rheumatism." What the physicians do not know on the subject would fill a far more portly tome than what they do know; and in studying this question in particular, one may appreciate to some degree what the frater- nity are compelled to combat in searching for light on obscure subjects. The disease may be palliated to a certain extent, but thus far all the painstaking researches of the sons of Æscula- pius have failed to exorcise it; and once in its clutches, the victim may hope for no absolute enfranchisement here below. The old Greeks vainly tried to conquer it, and as far back as the reign of Augustus it was written, *Tollere nodosam nescit medicina Podagram* (Medicine cannot remove the knotty Gout). The very name, " Gout ! " has a ferocious ferine sound, like the growl of some remorseless monster ready to fasten upon his prey. No other painful disease receives so little sympathy. " The toothach, the

The Malady

paine of the gowt, how grievous soever, because they kill not, who reckoneth them in the number of maladies ? " The sufferer from rheumatism is condoled with ; the victim of Gout is left to colchicum and his own consolation.

The disease was as well known in olden times as it is to-day; it was in fact more common among the old Romans than at present, when even with women it was of frequent occurrence. By the ancients it was looked upon as the daughter of Bacchus and Venus, a Greek epigram reading, " Of limb-relaxing Bacchus and limb-relaxing Venus is born a daughter, the limb-relaxing Gout." An old Latin adage embodies a kindred idea, *Bacchus pater, Venus mater, et Ira obstetrix Arthritides ;* while an ancient German paraphrase of the Greek sentiment reads, —

> "Vinum der Vater, Cœna die Mutter,
> Venus die Habamm', machen das Podagram."

Lastly, Cowper, at a later day, cries from his " sofa," of —

> " — pangs arthritic, that infest the toe
> Of libertine excess."

Meditations on Gout

It is essentially a disease of civilisation, being unknown among savage races, and rarely occurring among those who have exchanged a wild for a civilised life.

It has been referred to by very many Greek and Roman writers, including the "Father of Medicine" Hippocrates, Ovid, Celsus, Seneca, Pliny, Martial, Dioscorides, Aretæus, and Galen. Horace, in the seventh Satire of the second book, tells of old Volanerius, a great diner-out, who was so afflicted with Gout in his fingers that he could not throw the dice, and hired a man by the day to cast for him. Lucian has devoted two dialogues to the subject, — *Tragopodagra* and *Ocypus*, — in each of which Gout is one of the personæ, and to whom he assigns priests and ministers : —

"Who does not know me, Gout the unconquered, goddess
    of all earthly ills !
Whom neither the vapour of incense may placate,
Nor blood poured out on burning altars,
Nor the temple glowing with the suspended gifts of riches,
Whom neither Apollo, doctor of all gods celestial,
Nor the son of Apollo, the most learned Æsculapius, is
    able to expel."

The Malady

Indeed, its literature is abundant, both among ancient and modern writers; and colchicum was an incense offered it by Hippocrates and Galen, as well as at a later era by Sydenham and Watson. Who was the Dom Perignon to first discover the therapeutic virtues of the herb, has not been ascertained; and a monolith to the autumnal crocus — the hermodactyl and *anima articulorum* of antiquity — has therefore yet to be erected. Though comparatively little used until the latter part of the eighteenth century, it is known that its remedial properties were familiar to the herbalists and monks of the middle ages, that it was early employed by the Arabs as a specific for arthritic afflictions, and that its name was given it by the old Greeks, from Colchis in Asia Minor, — a country where it grew.

From its being usually attributed to luxury and close familiarity with the rarer products of the vine, Gout is sometimes supposed by the uninitiated to be a rather desirable companion than otherwise, — the acquaintance with which confers a certain title of distinction upon the possessor. This might hold good were it a necessary sequent of a faultless palate and the signet of a supreme judge of wine. But gastronomy and finesse of taste are often no auxiliaries in its acquisition; it may be acquired by ordinary beer and beefsteak as readily as by *Châteaubriands* and a well stocked wine-cellar. And, like Faust when he made a compact with Mephistopheles, Gout proves an equally rigorous task-master, who allows no turning back or renunciation of his allegiance. You may whistle him up readily, once his acquaintance has been made, but he obstinately refuses to be whistled down; he remains your most steadfast friend in the sense that he will never desert you. He appears when your habits are already formed, and when therefore they have become extremely difficult to change. The corrective or preventive, accordingly, rests largely with physicians and parents, rather than with him who eventually is to prove the sufferer, — in their apprising and advising him of the foe that may be lying in ambush amid the sauces, the bottles, the sweets, and the flesh-pots. Then if the avalanche falls, *tant pis* — the victim alone will be to blame. But in numerous cases, as statistics prove, the sufferer has little choice in the matter, and must perforce pay the penalty of the errors of his forefathers, who sowed the wind and had the pleasure, while he reaps the whirlwind and counts the pain. The preventive and cure, moreover, are difficult in all cases. It is hard to whip the lethargically disposed into exercise, and equally difficult to restrain those who are naturally so inclined from the pleasures of the table. The lesson, therefore, usually comes by experience, the sternest of teachers ; and in the case of Gout, experience generally comes too late.

In England, as compared with other countries, the malady was much more common during the three and four bottle days when Port was the staple liquid and great quantities of heavy viands were consumed ; though it is still more endemic as a heritage there to-day than elsewhere. One will recall Thomson's lines in *The Castle*

Meditations on Gout

of Indolence as especially pertinent to those times as well as to the characteristic torments of the seizure, —

"The sleepless Gout here counts the crowing cocks,
A wolf now gnaws him, now a serpent stings."

Contrasted with a century ago in England, an increase in the numbers affected, but a mitigation of the forms is noticeable, with these distinctions : a lessened frequency of the more severe manifestations, a milder type of the acute attack, and a greater predominance of conditions which may be described as " attenuations of Gout," or goutiness in which there may exist just enough of the articular trouble to identify their gouty origin and character. This change in type and severity may be attributed to the largely decreased consumption of heavy wines, notably Port; to the fact that hygiene has been made far more of a study than formerly; and that the enlightened advice of the physician has been better heeded. The advances of cookery in England, as well, have presumably not been without their good results. Notwithstanding all this, Gout remains remarkably prevalent and seemingly ineradicable in Great Britain. "Even the most critical observers," Ewart declares, "will probably agree in recognising not only an increased prevalence of gout and goutiness among the upper classes, but its wider extension to strata previously less affected." [1]

Hereditary predisposition, according to statistics, is accountable for the large majority of cases, Sir Charles Scudamore having computed 322 instances with a derivative tendency among over 500 subjects ; while of 80 cases reported to a Commission of the French Academy, in 34 the disease had been transmitted. Of these cases analysed by Scudamore with reference to age, in only 5 did the disease occur in persons under eighteen ; in 142 cases the ages at the time of the first occurrence were between twenty and thirty years; in 194 cases, between thirty and forty ; in 118, between forty and fifty ; in

[1] Dr. William Ewart, *Gout and Goutiness, and their Treatment.*

38, between fifty and sixty; and in only 10
cases, between sixty and sixty-six. In 341 out
of these cases, one or both great toes were
affected, to the exclusion of other joints; an
average fully confirmed by Garrod. In those
instances where Gout commences between
twenty and thirty, it is usually inherited. It is
further stated by Garrod that in some families
the inherited tendency is so strong that all their
members, whatever precautions they may adopt,
suffer from Gout; and in many English families
it has been handed down from father to son for
centuries; the tendency being much more frequently derived from the father's than the
mother's side.

Sir Leicester Dedlock, in *Bleak-House*, rises before one in strong confirmation of this statement,
when his faithful ally pinions him by both legs
in the old oak bed-chamber at Chesney Wold:
" All the Dedlocks, in the direct male line,
through a course of time during and beyond
which the memory of man goeth not to the
contrary, have had the gout. It has come down

through the illustrious line, like the plate, or the pictures, or the place in Lincolnshire. Hence Sir Leicester yields up his family legs to the family disorder, as if he held his name and fortune on that feudal tenure. He feels that for a Dedlock to be laid upon his back and spasmodically twitched and stabbed in his extremities, is a liberty taken somewhere; but he thinks, ' We have all yielded to this; it belongs to us; it has for some hundreds of years been understood that we are not to make the vaults in the park interesting on more ignoble terms.' "

Next to heredity, unquestionably the most important element in the ætiology and initiation of the disease is the patient's own mode of life; its development in this case being generally ascribed to luxury, an over-generous diet, and lack of adequate exercise; together with a latent proclivity to the gouty diathesis, or a certain predisposition from various causes in the individual.

A third and frequent factor is lead-poisoning, it having been observed that type-setters, plumbers, house-painters, and workers in lead-mills are particularly subject to the disease. This is far more the case in England than in foreign countries, and in London still more than in other cities of the kingdom, which leads to the belief that the disease is not so much the product of lead in itself as that the operation of certain gout-producing causes, less frequent elsewhere, is largely assisted by it. Its increased prevalence, particularly in the English metropolis, has accordingly been ascribed to the London workman's alimentation, — rather than to race or climatic conditions, — in which animal food, stout, and heavy ales figure to a large extent. It is noteworthy that in Scotland, Ireland, and the North, where spirits are much more freely used than stout and ale, Gout is far less common than in London and the South.

Numerous other causes, apart from heredity and alimentation, may be instrumental in producing or furthering the disease. Physical inertia, undue worry, taking cold, an accident to the foot or limb of a sensitive joint, a tight shoe, a sprain or strain, even sudden climatic changes and sudden changes of regimen, where the foundation for the malady is already laid, may incite an attack. Too violent exercise under similar conditions may likewise prove an exciting cause. Examples have occurred where bicycling has brought on a seizure, or where the use of the wheel has a tendency to irritate the part that has previously been affected, — a consequent which may be readily understood when it is considered how important a part the feet are called upon to perform in cycling. Excess of exercise, moreover, is attended with danger to the predisposed, inasmuch as it can suddenly increase the production of uric acid, the toxic properly of Gout, to such a degree that the kidneys are unable to excrete the amount produced.

Apart from these auxiliary causes, Dr. Meredeth Clymer's description of its pathology is most axiomatic and true: " A disordered digestion is the *primum mobile* of the whole train of morbid phenomena." Equally terse is John Mason Good's definition: " An entonic state of the vessels, joined with plethora, may be set down as the predisposing cause to acquired gout." " I believe the pathology of it," says Thomas K. Chambers, " to be a slight flux of mucus, deficient gastric secretion, and yet a vigorous, sometimes even excessive appetite. Hence such persons have not that check of failing desire for food which makes the meals of other invalids moderate, and eat more than their imperfect gastric juice can digest." To these opinions may be added the conclusion of Dr. Frederick C. Shattuck : " The most commonly accepted view as to its nature is that it depends upon defective oxidation, which may be brought about in two ways, — either by the ingestion of more food than can be properly oxidised, or by the presence of such conditions that even a moderate supply of food cannot be worked up and undergo its proper transformations, — a theory that will account for gout among the poor as well as the rich."

That it is not limited to the rich, and is not solely a patrician disease, has been abundantly proven. Friars who are fond of good living, butlers swollen with Burgundy, and dockmen plethoric with porter are cited as common examples; while not a few occur among the lower classes, with apparently no inciting cause. Like Horace's "pallida Mors," who knocks at lowly shed and regal tower, so Gout is confined to no classes or conditions, but occurs as an every-day malady.

Cullen's treatise on the subject is full of sententious observation; and despite some of his fallacies, probably no nineteenth-century writer has presented its ætiological features more concisely than has he in these paragraphs: —

"The occasional causes of the gout seem to be of two kinds: first, those which induce a plethoric state of the body; secondly, those which, in plethoric habits, induce a state of debility.

"Of the first kind are a sedentary, indolent manner of life, a full diet of animal food, and the large use of wine or of other fermented liquors. These circumstances commonly precede the disease.

"Of the second kind of occasional causes

which induce debility are, excess in venery; in-temperance in the use of intoxicating liquors; indigestion produced either by the quantity or quality of aliments; much application to study or business; night-watching; excessive evacua-tions; the ceasing of usual labour; the sudden change from a very full to a very spare diet; the large use of acids and acescents; and, lastly, cold applied to the lower extremities."[1]

To briefly emphasise its most frequent causes, it may be said that the general tendency of eating too rapidly and of charging the stomach with more than it can properly digest, are among the most predisposing agents. These, in connection with insufficient exercise and respiration, a gener-ous use of flesh food and alcoholic beverages, as also sweets and acids, and perhaps a lack of tone in some of the gastric functions or the organs of elimination, causes mal-assimilation, which with some induces dyspepsia, and with others assumes the form of Gout.

But although alcoholic beverages are a trench-

[1] *First Lines of the Practice of Physic* (1777).

ant instrument in challenging and provoking Gout, very many cases occur where the disease is not in the least dependent upon spirituous fluids. Generally, in such examples the patients have full appetites and are large eaters of animal food. Other examples, however, occur where the subjects are light consumers of flesh food, and whose appetites are merely normal. Where the disease occurs in such instances, it is more often derivative than acquired ; as in the case of not a few women who have directly inherited the diathesis, and directly encouraged it through their fondness for pastry and sweets. That sweets, noticeably in the form of saccharine wines, are most pernicious, will require no argument. And despite the fact that all kinds of saccharine substances are converted into a sugar known as glucose before they are assimilated and absorbed, yet the system refuses to countenance the glucose of commerce as a substitute for the natural form. It is for this reason that candies are especially objectionable to the digestive organs, glucose being largely employed in their manufacture. In a bulletin issued on "Foods and Food Adulterants" by the Department of Agriculture, it is stated that not a single sample of twenty-five candies examined consisted of pure cane sugar, being all mixtures of cane sugar with commercial glucose, or starch, or both.

To how great a degree a neurotic condition or temperament may influence the disease has been comparatively little dwelt upon. But when it is considered how many diseases are directly furthered by such a condition, like urticaria for example, with which Gout is often associated, it will be readily seen that a nervous habit may exercise a strong predisposing influence, and merit the ætiological importance it is assigned by Sir Willoughby Wade : " The nervous system is largely concerned in all the phases of gout and of goutiness; and probably it also influences their mysterious hereditary transmission." [1] " We may assume with Rendu," Ewart also observes, " that while the original fault lies with nutrition and with digestion, the nervous system has an

[1] *On Gout as a Peripheral Neurosis* (1893).

undoubted influence on the metabolic exchanges and on assimilation, and that it also exercises a determining influence upon some of the acute phenomena. But there is no adequate proof that the nervous system is independently and primarily responsible for the production of gout. We must own, however, that the subtle mechanism of these influences is still unexplained. It is no less mysterious than the mechanism by which the occurrence of a severe articular attack often frees the patient from his previous ill-health."

As opposed to the charges of high-living and intemperance made by vegetarians, Grahamites, and intemperate tea and water devotees, it is time that Gout should be clearly defined for what it really is in very many instances, — a perverse, ungrateful, maleficent malady, that delights upon the slightest pretext in assaulting vulnerable humanity at the most unseasonable hours and inconvenient times; an infliction that is especially prone to picket club-men, physicians, poets, and heads of official departments;

Meditations on Gout

a stomachic metabasis that in some indeterminable, underhanded way is occasionally connected with the moderate use of certain wines and malt-liquors, though these be otherwise of an innocuous character; a scourge that for the most part is beyond the prevention of the average sufferer who duly follows the laws of the decalogue and leads the customary life of civilisation; an abnormal affliction depending in a marked degree upon constitutional tendency and normal instinct, as well as occupation, climate, and various other abettors more or less impossible to circumvent; and, lastly, a stealthy, rancorous, irascible, mordacious disorder, masked under many forms, that continues to defy the science, skill, and pharmacopœia of the medical profession. It is the charlock of maladies, that may thrive in every soil and will not be eradicated, — the Wolf of diseases, with ensanguined fangs and encarmined jowl, who refuses to be baited even with asafœtida.

Selecting for its victims subjects of all temperaments and widely divergent conditions, it

The Malady

attacks the comparatively young, the middle-aged, and the old; it fastens upon the man of robust constitution equally with him of frail habit; it invades the home of the scholar, and prisons Plutus in his bed. Cruel and relentless, it strikes the professor at his desk, the general in his camp, the judge upon his bench. Its poison comes by heritage, its venom lurks in the wine-cup, its seeds are sown at the gatherings of good-cheer. Emperors and kings have known its power, doctors and surgeons felt its lance, pontiffs have groaned in its grasp; while the priest, the monk, and red-robed cardinal have roared with pain when crushed within its clamp of steel. Only woman is comparatively exempt from its inflictions, though she on her part is a greater sufferer from its more merciless relative, capsular rheumatism or rheumatic gout.[1]

---

[1] *At vero (quod mihi aliisque licet, tam fortunæ quam ingenii dotibus mediocriter instructis, hoc morbo laborantibus solatio esse possit) ita vixerunt atque ita tandem mortem obierunt magni Reges, Dynastæ exercituum classiumque, Duces, Philosophi, aliique, his similes haud pauci. Verbo*

Meditations on Gout

With respect to pathology, medical authorities are unanimous in pronouncing the characteristic feature of Gout, as distinguished from other affections of the locomotive apparatus, like rheumatic gout and various forms of rheumatism, to consist in the periodicity of the gouty paroxysm. It may also induce numerous other derangements in the internal economy, which may assume either a periodic or a continuous type. These derangements may start from the onset, or they may, and more generally do, not occur until a series of attacks of regular Gout. Its first appearance in-

dicam, articularis hicce morbus (quod vix de quovis alio adfirmaveris) divites plures intermit quam pauperes, plures sapientes quam fatuos. —SYDENHAM, "Tractatus de Podagra et Hydrope" (1683).

But indeed (and this may be comforting to me and others but little endowed with either money or brains who are afflicted with this disease) in this manner have lived, and in this manner have finally died, majestic Kings, Rulers, Generals, Philosophers, and Admirals, and many others of like rank. Briefly, I should assert that this Gout (and you can hardly affirm as much of any other malady) slays more of the Rich than the Poor, and rather the Wise than the Fool. —SYDENHAM, *Treatise on Gout and Dropsy* (1683).

variably occurs in the acute form, generally followed by a longer or shorter period of renewed health; and not until the system has become undermined by repeated assaults or unless one be specially predisposed, does it merge into the chronic or atonic form, as also what are termed the retrocedent and aberrant forms. Although its manifestations are infinitely varied in all its types, in nearly three-fourths of the total number of examples the first attack is confined to the large joint or metatarso-phalangeal joint of one of the great toes; the left, according to Dr. Gairdner, being more often chosen than the right. Hence the term *Podagra*, or Gout of the foot; as also *Gonagra*, that of the knee; *Chiragra*, the hand; *Omagra*, the shoulder; *Ischiagra*, the hip; and *Rhachisagra*, the invertebral joints.

While death rarely occurs from the disease in its regular type, complete recovery is an anomaly; the chronic form, however, with the various complications that frequently attend it, after a variable number of years usually becomes fatal. Spring and Autumn are the most common seasons of incursion in all varieties of the malady. With *Aries* it ushers in the vernal equinox, and with *Sagittarius* proclaims the reign of frost and snow : —

> "— the fall of the leaf and the starting of the bud
> Are the seasons he loves by the door;
> Then his blood begins to rouse, this Caliban I house,
> And it's 'Wolf, wolf, wolf !' at the door."

"The wherefore I know not" is the brief answer Dr. Trousseau makes to these its chosen times of visitation. The reason, indeed, seems as inexplicable, physiologically, as that lame girls should invariably possess surpassingly lovely complexions.

Not that it is thus condescending on the start, by any means, and that it insists upon a semi-yearly visit. Far from it ; it has plenty of patients to keep it from feeling lonely. To be so frequent a guest, it requires much petting on the part of the palate and stomach; and only after many months of waiting, which may even be extended to a period of two or three years, does it deign to pay its respects anew, and help to free the blood of its impurities with its stylet and its drill. After repeated seizures, if its admonitions be not heeded, it proceeds to pass from the toe to the knee-joint, the knuckles, and other portions of the body, where it leaves its grim souvenirs in the shape of certain petrifactions known as chalk-stones, which take place around and outside the joint, filling up the areolar tissue, and lying in general immediately beneath the skin. Thus where the disease continues to make progress, numerous joints become involved, several of which may be simultaneously affected, or affected during the same attack. Anchylosis in a painful form distorts the hands and fingers, together with implications of internal organs, or inflammations of tissues — permanent or periodic — other than those pertaining to the joints. In place of the foot, the stomach may be attacked, with distressing consequences to the entire system; or even the brain or heart may be seized upon, with death as the result.

Besides the manifold varieties of Gout itself, all eager to charge upon one at the slightest provocation, there exist numerous varieties of goutiness,

Meditations on Gout

or conditions of imperfectly declared Gout, in which various functional derangements of a general nature, not necessarily associated with defined structural changes, are present and threatening. Having its seat in the stomach and preying upon the frailties of that organ, goutiness is to be suspected in nearly all manner of stomachic disturbances; and who may declare himself free from some form of mal-assimilation or of mal-elimination? Goutiness may harbour in dyspepsia, it may lurk in indigestion, it may be present in flatulency, it may hover over many minor gastric disorders. So that in nearly every case of indigestion, biliousness, and stomach trouble, the subject may have cause to fear the evil, and justly surmise that the foe is already undermining, plotting, and making ready for the assault.

Above all, where there is the least disposition to puffiness of the feet, or where the ankles, instep, great toe, or any portion of the lower extremities are sensitive, tender, or readily responsive to atmospheric influences, goutiness is to be mistrusted, and the patient were wise to be instantly upon his guard. To be sure, it may be merely rheumatism that is indicated; but rheumatism and Gout are often so closely allied that it is a very difficult matter to draw the distinction; and one can ill afford to dally with any indications of goutiness, lest they develop into the greater evil. Abstinence and Carlsbad, at the start, are the safest means of mitigating the penalty of dining, and indulgence in strawberries and oat-meal. For it must be remembered that before Gout can appear, goutiness must be present, and that uric acid, the toxic property of Gout, already exists even in the normal condition of the blood. Man, therefore, is born with a distinct gouty tendency, aggravated through the dietetic misdeeds of his ancestors, and furthered by his own voluntary or involuntary lapses. In other words, the fire is in readiness, and awaits but the striking of the tinder. How, then, may one expect to escape, unless by constant vigilance and the most subtle discrimination in the choice of a doctor, as well as in the selection of foods and beverages?

That a person afflicted with Gout should

receive little sympathy, except from his physician or from his fellow-sufferers, is scarcely to be wondered at, in view of the opinion that the disease is a just punishment to the offender, — a case where " just disease to luxury succeeds." The very nature of the malady, at least to those who have it not, provokes a smile. To think that a bottle of wine or a truffled paté, or even a glass of beer, instead of being absorbed and eliminated by the system in the usual manner, should mine its way through the thighs, knees, calves, ankles, and instep, to explode at last in a fiery volcano in one's great toe, seems a mirth-provoking phenomenon to all but him who is immediately concerned. Almost equally strange, too, is the period selected by the visitant for its assault, — the silent watches of the night, when it rouses the victim from his slumbers, and the softest bed becomes a veritable rack of torture. The pains invariably come on *inter canem et lupum,* or that time when the dog has gone to sleep, and the wolf has started upon his nocturnal rounds. They diminish towards dawn, —

The Malady

sub galli cantu, at the crowing of the cock, as
Sydenham has chronicled. In vain your moans
of anguish as the awl, the gimlet, and probe of
the Inquisitor are thrust into your very bone and
marrow. You might as well implore mercy
from the Iron Virgin of the *Burg* of Nürnberg,
or seek flight if locked in the dungeon of Chillon.
It reminds one of " The Red Wolf " of Carman :

" In the dread 'one of the night I can hear him snuff the sill ;
　　Then it 's ' Wolf, wolf, wolf ! ' at the door :
His damned persistent bark, like a husky's in the dark,
　　His ' Wolf, wolf, wolf ! ' at the door.

' I have tried to rid the house of the mis-begotten spawn ;
　　But he skulks like a shadow by my door,
With the same uncanny glee as when he came to me
　　With his first cry of ' Wolf ! ' at my door.

" But when the night is old, and the stars begin to fade,
　　And silence walks the path by my door,
Then is his dearest hour, his most unbridled power,
　　And low comes his ' Wolf ! ' at the door.

" I turn me in my sleep between the night and day,
　　While dreams throng the yard at my door,
In my strong soul aware of a grewsome terror there,
　　Soon to knock with command at my door ! " [1]

　　　　[1] Bliss Carman; *Behind the Arras.*

3　　　　　　　33

Meditations on Gout

It is unnecessary to describe more at length the pangs of the acute paroxysm, — *nunc tensionem violentam vel ligamentorum dilacerationem, nunc morsum canis rodentis quandoque pressuram et coarctationem exprimens.* All those who have experienced them assuredly need no memoranda to bring them vividly to mind. Those who have not may be referred to Sydenham's account, — a description founded on personal experience of life-long duration, and the most graphic that has yet appeared upon the subject.

THE THEORY

THE THEORY.

The history of human opinion is scarcely anything more than the history of human errors. — VOLTAIRE.

AVING referred thus briefly to the history, ætiology, and pathology, the theory of the disorder is next to claim attention. By all, it is recognised that when its distinguishing features — the gouty deposits — already exist, there is present a morbid condition of the blood and humours, a fact equally understood by the ancients. It remained for modern research to discover the precise nature of this poisonous element, when Wollaston (1797), Tennant, Fourcroy, and others traced it to an accumulation of uric acid in the system, — a uric-acid dyscrasia. About 1787–1793 Murray Forbes, noting the close connection between Gout and gravel, and the proneness of the disorder to

37

form concretions, attributed Gout to the presence of *Lithisiac,* or what has since been termed lithic or uric acid. To Wollaston, however, is generally attributed the discovery of the active poison.

In 1848 Sir A. Garrod showed that in Gout the blood contains an excess of this element, and that its excretion by the kidneys is diminished. Numerous investigations have been undertaken since then; but while many well established facts relating to this theory have occurred, we do not know why the normal chemical processes are disturbed, and are unable to explain the connection between the various phenomena observed.[1] It is concluded that in Gout there exists so large a disproportion between the rate at which this acid is formed and that at which it is eliminated, as to cause it to accumulate in the blood to an extent beyond the solvent capacity of that fluid; or else that the solvent power of the blood itself is, for some reason or other, diminished.[2]

Garrod is inclined to the former opinion,

[1] Prof. Adolph Strümpell.　　[2] Prof. H. Senator.

believing, in common with most of the faculty, that the action of the kidneys is disturbed at a very early period, thereby promoting a surplus of uric acid in the blood. It is in the serum of the blood, he further states, that the chief deviation from the healthy standard is discovered, and in this portion it is not so much that the normal constituents are affected as that excretory substances which should have been eliminated are retained, — an effect due to the imperfect action of certain of the excreting organs, more especially the kidneys. It is supposed by some that the spleen, if not at the bottom of the trouble, nevertheless plays a very important rôle in the formation of uric acid, in that it is liable to enlargement when the products of gastro-intestinal digestion are being absorbed ; and consequently a corresponding increase is observable in the amount of this acid eliminated several hours after a meal.

Yet excess of this morbid element is not all : disturbances of digestion in themselves contributing to generate organic acids (lactic acid, volatile fatty acids) in abundance ; and it is clear that these acids, becoming absorbed, may diminish the alkalinity of the blood.[1]   Over eating and drinking frequently cause undue production of other acids during digestion, which take the place of uric acid and prevent its elimination.[2]   It would seem that during certain forms of disease, new poisons, which are extremely virulent in their action, are produced by modified chemical changes. It is probable that poisoning so induced is much more common than is generally supposed.[3]   We neither know whether the uric acid diathesis be the primary and chief anomaly in Gout, and whether it be not accompanied by other and more important changes in the composition of the blood; nor do we know the disturbances of nutrition by which one of the constant products of normal nutrition, uric acid, is formed in excess.[4]

It is now conceded that acid, not necessarily uric, is responsible for a very large number of the

---

[1] Prof. H. Senator.
[2] Dr. Frederick T. Roberts.
[3] Dr. Benjamin Ward Richardson.
[4] Dr. Felix von Niemeyer.

derangements of health which are manifested in many different ways; among which may be mentioned neuralgia, headache, migraine, myalgia, dyspepsia, skin diseases, acute inflammation, arterial and renal diseases, and various lung and bowel troubles.[1]

But whatever the existing, immediate, or combined causes of the morbific influences may be, it is the general opinion that the malady is a direct result of this redundance in the arterial and venous channels of the system, either introduced from without or generated from within, which, not finding its natural exits to the degree that it should, becomes deposited as urate of soda in the affected tissues, just as in rheumatism an excess of lactic acid occurs. So far as the resemblance between Gout and rheumatism is concerned, the former is much more closely related to a dyspeptic condition; and while rheumatism first attacks the shoulders or elbows, Gout nearly always selects for its onset the ball of the foot. Nevertheless, according to Trousseau, there are many so-called

[1] Dr. Albert Harris Hoy.

metastases of rheumatism which are nothing else
than metastases of Gout ;[1] or, as Flint expresses
it, Gout and rheumatism may be said to belong to
the same family, but each has a separate individuality.[2]   By some authorities, including Charcot
and Haig, an arthritic diathesis is believed in,
equally predisposing to either, the event being
determined in each instance by the special circumstances of the attack.   Indeed, Hutchinson expresses the opinion that Gout is but rarely of pure
breed, and often a complication of rheumatism.
It so often mixes itself up with rheumatism, and
the two in hereditary transmission become so intimately united, that it is a matter of considerable
difficulty to ascertain how far rheumatism pure
can go.[8]   Rendu is of the opinion that acute
Gout in the joints is, like acute rheumatic arthri-
tis, often traceable to an impression of cold, and
that this must operate through some nervous en-

[1] Dr. A. Trousseau, *Lectures on Clinical Medicine.*
[2] Dr. Austin Flint, *A Treatise on the Principles and Practice of Medicine.*
[8] Dr. J. Hutchinson, *Pedigree of Disease.*

ergy. Rheumatism more often assails the poor, and Gout the well-to-do. Both conditions are the products of fermentation, and may be the sequel of a hyper-production, or of a diminished elimination, — the prevailing belief being that it is more the result of defective elimination than of over-production. Both are acid diseases, marked by changes in the alkalinity of the blood ; both are frequently hereditary ; and the dietetic regulations to be observed in their treatment are virtually the same.

Briefly summarised, it may be said that acquired Gout, and very often the transmitted form, are caused by the ingestion of food or fluids or both, to a greater extent than the eliminating capacities of the system can provide for, — whether this lack of elimination be the result of a deficiency in some of the excreting organs, or the consequence of a surplusage of nourishment. Finally, the diathesis may also be induced by an inadequacy of gastric secretion to perform the proper functions of digestion, or too rapid eating which acts as an equally disturbing element.

Meditations on Gout

" We recognise that Gout does not take its genesis solely in port wine and gluttony," but on the contrary may have its origin in many causes the exact nature of which is often a puzzle to the diagnostician. For a concise summary of the uric acid diathesis as viewed by various authorities, the reader may be referred with advantage to a small volume by Dr. F. Levison of Copenhagen.[1]

A table of statistics of Gout compiled from.the different countries of the world, were it obtainable, might diffuse some interesting light on the theme. Next to England, Holland is said to be most subject to the malady ; the Dutchman being an excellent connoisseur of wine, as well as of *Schnapps* and " blue and white." No doubt the dampness of the Netherlands is also a promoter. Gout, as already stated, is quite common in certain portions of Germany, more so in Bavaria than others ; a fact in which climatic conditions — sudden changes induced by the close proximity of the Alps and the Böhmer Wald — may play

[1] *The Uric Acid Diathesis, Gout, Sand and Gravel* (London, 1894).

a part; but for which malt liquor must be held principally responsible. Yet when one considers the enormous quantity of beer consumed in Germany, the rivers of *Hof, Franziskaner, Augustiner, Pschorr, Erlanger, Würtzburger, Nürnberger, Augsburger, Pilsener,* and *Bräus* innumerable that are hourly poured by the *Maas* and *litre* down the throats of thirsty millions, it would seem that this agent is far less deleterious there than in other countries, — an assumption that would point to the much more wholesome and finished quality of the national beverage, or to its better combination with the customary alimentation, or to both conditions.

The excellence of German beer is proverbial; the quality of hops and malt and water, the slight amount of alcohol it contains, and its absolute purity. Certainly there is no comparison between the light, refreshing brews of Germany as drunk upon the spot — beverages adapted solely for rapid consumption — and the heady, heavy beers and bitter pale ales of Great Britain, or the adulterated products of the United States. It is

Meditations on Gout

well known that many among the poorer classes of
Germany subsist largely upon bread and beer, or
more correctly speaking, upon beer and bread, and
that the national beverage is generously given to
children from infancy, with no qualms of a future
uric-acid diathesis. Racial conditions would hardly
seem to enter as a qualifying component, unless
it is that the Germans are more prone to lead an
out-of-door life than the English ; for the Teuton,
though extremely fond of greens and vegetables,
is a large consumer of meat in the form of veal,
pork, and sausages ; and with the exception of
his leisurely *Spaziergangs* or walks that Schiller
extols, does not follow outside sports as vigor-
ously as do many other nationalities. But he has
only to enter one of his attractive beer-gardens to
find himself virtually out-of-doors, and to enjoy
with " Lust " the " freie Luft," and his cool,
foaming glass. Here amid genial companion-
ship and the cadences of dulcet strings and reeds,
he may scatter care to the winds, and with no
thought of life's ailments join in the joyous refrain of *Der Wildschütz* : —

The Theory

Heiterkeit und Fröhlichkeit,
Ihr Götter dieses Lebens,
Euch zu sehen, zu erflehen,
Ist das Ziel des Strebens!

The argument advanced by wine-drinkers, that in those countries where wine is largely consumed, Gout is seldom met with, requires to be taken with considerable allowance. Relatively, this is the case. But while it is true that, in proportion to the amount consumed, most wine countries are comparatively free from the malady, it by no means follows that they are exempt from Gout, gravel, and diabetes. In a certain measure the same hygienic and dietetic conditions hold good for all. Thus the Parsees of India who are great meat-eaters are afflicted with Gout, which very rarely occurs in tropical climates. And in France the *gourmet* and wine-drinker who leads a more or less sedentary life, does not escape the penalty, even in Bordeaux where he may drink the lightest of French wine at the fountain-head. Of late years diabetes has increased largely in France. Among the luxurious

47

class, and in Bordeaux perhaps more than in other places in the republic, this disease has become extremely common, as stated by Dr. Carles, the well-known local Professor of the Faculty of Medicine. " The Bordelais," he says, " is by nature and his environment extremely fond not only of good wines, but also of the fine dishes with which they are injuriously accompanied. As the nature of his business, in addition, necessitates a sedentary life and constant preoccupation, he finds himself more than otherwise afflicted with diabetes, gout, and kindred maladies common to the well-to-do." [1]

Considered from the standpoint of the experience of various countries, it again appears that food and drink, luxury, temperament, climate, hereditary disposition, insufficient oxygenation and out-of-door exercise; or in many instances, to speak more truly, a combination of some of these conditions, are the fundamental elements that incite and develop the disease; and that while extremely protean in its forms and the con-

[1] Dr. P. Carles, *Le Pain des Diabétiques.*

ditions which induce it, it everywhere owes its origin to causes more or less alike, within or without the control of the individual, and within or without the power of the physician to remedy.

It may yet be queried, on the other hand, how far various local and racial conditions may enter as mitigating or operative agents. The relative health of nations, the question of natural temperament, climate, occupations, diversions, and general mode of life, are factors to be considered. Were the phlegmatic Teuton to give up his *Gerstensaft* and devote himself to the consumption of Haut-Médoc, or were the impressible Gaul to accompany his *entrées* with *Münchner*, the arthritic result might be painful to contemplate ; the fate of nations depending not only "upon what they are fed," but in equal measure upon the congruous liquid accompaniment of their food. No one has yet called attention to the fact that woman may be instrumental in the evolution of the malady. Had Eve never tempted Adam with a raw sub-acid fruit; did Circe not constantly tender the "wine-cup" which she is

4

credited with presenting; were women not so gluttonous of sweets, and consequently largely responsible in developing and transmitting a uric-acid diathesis; had Bacchus no attendant nymphs to replenish his chalice — all might be different! It will be readily apparent, therefore, that the subject of Gout — its subtle causes and its remedy — does not enter so much in the domain of the physician as in the province of the pantologist, metaphysician, and philosopher; and in place of the Sydenhams and Garrods, should be turned over to such minds as Goethe, Schopenhauer, and Spencer for its true elucidation.

Man proverbially eats more than he can properly assimilate; and leaving the stronger wines and heavy malt-liquors out of the question, the disease would appear to be generated fully as much from food as from alcoholic fluids; heavy viands being certainly one of its most active operating agents. Although France is noted for the excellence of its cuisine as well as for its large consumption of wine, Gout prevails to a very much less extent there than in England.

The Theory

The same is true of Germany compared to the
latter country. This fact may be due to a plural-
ity of reasons. Firstly, through a less strong
hereditary tendency influenced primarily by Port
and heavy ales; secondly, through the lesser
consumption of animal foods, and the use of a
more mixed diet; thirdly, to the lighter and
superior cookery; fourthly, to the skilful use of
herbs and seasonings in cooking, which, judi-
ciously employed, stimulate the gastric secretions
and facilitate digestion; and, lastly, to the pleasing variety of aliments, and the custom of serving
them in dainty limited courses which renders
rapid eating virtually a *tour de force*. In this
manner, especially as the meals are accompanied
by a light, refreshing wine, the palate is pleased
and the stomach is less fatigued. " In our case,"
says the Frenchman, addressing the Englishman,
we have ' goût ' for the taste; in your case, you
have ' gout ' for the result."

Among the labouring classes and less well-to-
do classes of the provinces where much wine or
cider, and some beer is consumed, the diet is

necessarily plain; but the wines, whether white or red, are always wholesome and never over-rich. Of late years Gout has become much more prevalent in the Eastern and Middle States of America than formerly, from the same main reasons that induce it in other countries. American beer, very much of which is far from being confined to hops and malt and water, has been assigned by many physicians a foremost place as a promoter of the malady. " The question of the adulteration of beer, in this country at least," says Dr. Hoy, " is one the importance of which can scarcely be overestimated. Any physician who has had occasion to prescribe American beer must have been struck with its proneness to cause fermentation and gastric disturbance, while the use of imported beer is not followed by these results. The enormous consumption of glucose and powdered rice by brewers is a sufficient commentary on the purity of their goods."[1]

That vigorous exercise in the open air alone, when other strong inciting causes exist, is not a

[1] Dr. Albert Harris Hoy, *Eating and Drinking.*

The Theory

sure preventive is apparent when one considers
the case of England, where all forms of out-of-
door sports are more in vogue than in any other
country. " A man is a doctor or a fool at forty,"
saith a Spanish adage. But govern himself as he
may, within reasonable bounds, if his temperament be strongly predisposed, he will always find
it a difficult matter to forefend the uric-acid
diathesis, which has generally commenced its subtle inroads long before the fifth decade. Nevertheless, sufficient stress cannot be laid upon the
importance of exercise, oxygen, and sunlight, as
combined in an open-air life or a number of
hours spent every day out-of-doors, in the direct
tonical effect upon the general health, and thus in
the direct benefit to digestion and assimilation.

Some mode of attaining the advantages of this
form of hygiene should be sought by all those
whose occupations are of a confining or sedentary
character. The writer, the scholar, the lawyer,
the business-man, each and all, should have their
recreations that will lead them out-of-doors.
They should be familiar with Walton and White,

Meditations on Gout

Thoreau and Jefferies, in order to attain a fuller understanding of the delights and resources of Nature, even if they forego Hugh Miller, and "The Prelude" of Wordsworth. Nature stands smiling without, the same year by year, as each season proffers its countless charms. And to commune closely with her, if not always an antidote, is at any rate a prophylactic of great value in many disorders that molest mankind. Well for him who knows and loves her truly, and who may himself exemplify the poet's lines : —

> "The meanest floweret of the vale,
> The simplest note that swells the gale,
> The common sun, the air, the skies,
> To him are opening paradise."

To prescribe simply a certain number of miles in daily walks does not answer. This manner of exercise without a purpose, or rather a pleasure, connected with it, soon becomes irksome, and the walks gradually become shorter or are for the most part discontinued. One requires an incentive, — the rod to spur him to the waterside, the gun to open up the covers, the love of the

The Theory

botanist, ornithologist, or entomologist to draw him to the fields and woods. Or it may be equestrian exercise, the golf link, or the wheel, — any diversion that will lead one into the open air.

It is patent to all that the function of respiration is a double one, a sort of "give and take" affair, — receiving oxygen, and bartering therefor carbonic acid, precisely the reverse of what takes place in vegetation. It is easily deduced that retention of carbonic acid in the system is highly deleterious, even poisonous, and that its expulsion through the air passages, and its replacement by oxygen, is vital. Oxygenation of blood is revivifying, and furthers, directly and indirectly, all vital processes in the way of tissue-building, and activity of all emunctory organs; that is, elimination of effete matters from the body. To inhale as much pure air as possible, and check the retention of carbonic acid in the system, is a *sine qua non* in the treatment of many diseased conditions, and this applies to Gout *par excellence.* Thus it may be affirmed that whatever tends to the general health helps to prevent and expel disease; and hence open-air exercise, through increased respiration, cutaneous elimination, and its invigorating effects upon the appetite and digestive organs, becomes of signal importance in Gout.

Between Gout and dyspepsia, it has already been noted, there are certain features in common; though were one of the two maladies to be chosen, except where Gout assumes the chronic form, Gout would seem to be the lesser evil. Little is heard of Gout compared to the harrowing plaint of the confirmed dyspeptic, whose sufferings are written in every lineament. No wonder that Carlyle was vituperative and constantly showing his teeth. To quote his own words, "the accursed hag dyspepsia had got him bitted and bridled, and was ever striving to make his living walking day a thing of ghastly nightmare." But though in a certain sense the diseases are so dissimilar, they yet have many traits in common. "The more closely I have thought upon gout," Sydenham has stated, "the more I have referred it to indigestion." Each has its seat in the stomach or in the intestinal digestive tract, and each is the result of perverted assimilation. But the one, while excruciatingly painful for the time, is intermittent, whereas the other is more or less unintermitting; and Gout, except in hereditary examples, rarely occurs during early youth.

Stomachic disturbances such as flatulency, gastric fermentation, constipation, and the like, are almost always an accompaniment of each. Rich indeed is he, therefore, who has inherited and maintained a good digestion; for the stomach is the great seat and dispenser of joy, and one of the first requisites to sound health, without which all other joys must pale. But with the abuse that is so often heaped upon it by both the knowing and unknowing, the wonder is that it submits with half the grace it does; and like the harp that Watts sings of in the well-known hymn, strange it is that its

> "— thousand strings
> Should keep in tune so long."

Perfect health, which is above riches and for which riches often strives in vain, is seldom maintained throughout life, and is oftener a heritage of those whose lot compels them to expend bodily exertion and manual labour in the attainment of their daily needs than of those who bask in affluence or live in luxurious ease.

Riches proverbially begets its ills; and poverty, as distinguished from indigence and want, even if it have its thorns, is not altogether without its roses in that it is a preventive of many diseases that wealth invites. One is not apt to miss that with which he is unfamiliar; and the frugal fare of the labourer, earned by the expenditure of his muscle and his brawn, may, after all, possess a keener relish than the highly seasoned dishes of the epicure.[1] And as one must earnestly have coveted " that whereof he would enjoy an absolute delight," so it is one of Nature's laws that one must earn his physical well-being and the pleas-

[1] Many rich men, I dare boldly say it, that lie on down-beds, with delicacies pampered every day, in their well-furnished houses, live at less heart's ease, with more anguish, more bodily pain, and through their intemperance more bitter hours, than many a prisoner or galley-slave. (*The Anatomy of Melancholy.*)

The Theory

ure of living by some disbursement of physical exercise or physical toil.

As to the prognosis of the malady, it may be of comfort to some to know that concerning the individual paroxysm the following indications may be considered favourable : the limitation to few joints, or, better still, to one joint only, especially if that joint be a toe; acute fever, severe local inflammation, with great pain; strict periodicity of occurrence. The more marked all these features, the better is the prospect of unbroken health to follow the attack, and the longer may the period be expected to last. In other words the disease will be less apt to assume a chronic form, or end in chalk-stones and an attack upon the stomach and the heart. The prognosis of hereditary Gout is usually less hopeful than that of the acquired disease, the former being more obstinate and more prone to pass into the irregular variety.[1] Among other schedules, Richardson has presented the following

[1] Prof. H. Senator, *Diseases of the Locomotive Apparatus.*

59

table relating to the periods of mortality in general diseases of constitutional type: —

London.	GOUT.
Maximum.	Middle of March to end of April.
Minimum.	Beginning of June to end of year; absolute, September. A large increase takes place in last week in year. Another in middle of March ushering in annual maximum.[1]

Sydenham and Cullen have maintained that the disease is incurable, holding to the doctrine of non-interference, and " patience and flannel." "As for a radical cure," Sydenham declares, " one altogether perfect, and one whereby the patient might be freed from even the disposition to the disease — this lies, like Truth, *at the bottom of a well ;* and so deep is it in the innermost recesses of nature, that I know not when or by whom it will be brought forward into the light of day." Garrod believes that Gout in its acute form is as controllable as any other inflammatory affection, and that chronic Gout may be relieved to the extent of enabling the

---

[1] Benjamin Ward Richardson, *The Field of Disease.*

patient to enjoy life. Ewing, and some others, lean to a similar opinion. " Prior to its earliest warnings and for some time afterwards," says Ewing, " the remedy is in our own hands; an active and frugal life is a safe preventive, and may often be a cure."

In brief, by entirely changing one's mode of life and dietary, the disease may be possibly prevented if taken in its initial stages, and undoubtedly checked to a considerable extent in many of its later periods. A dullard may become rich by avoiding nearly all disbursements and pinching himself to the verge of starvation; nearly all is possible to persistent and rigid denial. One may also combat Gout on similar terms, and escape with a few flesh wounds. By converting the dinner into a frugal lunch or still more frugal supper, together with the leading of an open-air life, and the abstention from all alcoholic beverages, there is no doubt that Gout may be kept within reasonable bounds. *Per contra*, it may be said that life is worth living, and that there are things which are so good in them-

Meditations on Gout

selves that they are cheaply purchased by a little malady, if not by a little mortality. And of fret and cark and tribulation, to nearly every one is meted out his share. Life is short at its longest, and, after all, Omar's philosophy has a soothing sound : —

> " Ah, fill the cup ! What boots it to repeat
>   How time is slipping underneath our feet ?
> Unborn To-morrow and dead Yesterday,
>   Why fret about them if To-Day be sweet ? "

But all the wise and weighty observations of the sages, buried as they are in ponderous tomes in the *terra incognita* of the doctor's shelves, are mostly unknown and inaccessible to the lay-man in whom the seeds of the disease may be lurking or already germinating. And thus, unwarned and unarmed, knowing no more of the malady than that it has occurred to others, in entire unconsciousness of what the future holds in store, the rap of the Inquisitor comes, and the demon enters one's sleeping-chamber to claim him for his own. Were physicians true philan-thropists, they would early warn such of their patients as they considered in the category of "suspects," of the dangers and inconveniencies of the disease, even to placing Sydenham's monograph of the subject in their hands. Or, certainly, upon a first attack, they would thoroughly apprise, exhort, and instruct them regarding the coming events that already cast their shadows before. They should at once acquaint themselves with the foibles of their patient, — his hours and habits, his pet tipples and favourite dishes and sauces, even to demanding the open sesame of his wine-cellar, in order to ferret out the liquid offender.

Yet through the neglect of their bodily advisers who merely apply a temporary balm, the sufferer does not realise the seriousness of the evil until it has advanced to such an extent that remedies are of slight avail. Beyond certain stomachic disturbances of a more strongly marked character than usual, the patient has little warning of the first seizure; and this warning he knows not how to interpret aright. The advances are stealthy and insidious, and not

of a nature to excite alarm. Were the first
excesses or carelessness to visit the offender in
a mild form of retribution; or were there a
pronounced caution — a loud whistle of danger
ahead! for pains and penalties that are to follow,
he would at once begin the work of reformation,
and hasten to make terms with his stomach at
whatever cost.

Yet some there are who after having experienced a first seizure, may presage a threatened
attack by certain well-defined indices, — like
those portents in the sky that herald the approaching storm. The low growl of the thunder
is heard ere the lightning's shaft descends. Wise
is he who heeds the admonition, and adopts
heroic measures to avoid the crisis if he can.
Previous to an attack, as already observed, there
is frequently indigestion of some standing, accompanied by acidity and a furred tongue;
together with other premonitory signs, especially disturbances of the nervous system with
which the malady is frequently closely allied.
The appetite is capricious, the muscles may be-

come cramped in the lower extremities and calves of the leg, sleep is not sound, tobacco loses its flavour, and wine its bouquet. The physical functions become more or less dulled, there is an inaptitude for intellectual labour, and the system lacks in elasticity and tone. These, one and all, are the mares'-tails, streamers, mackerel-clouds and primrose-bands that point to the impending change. Among the infinite peculiarities of the malady, none, perhaps, is more strange than the hearty appetite and minutely fine appreciation of the bouquet and savour of wines which often *immediately* precede an attack, after a period of capricious or failing appetite, and more or less obtuse discrimination of customary food. The golden or terra-cotta rim of a glass of ripe Bordeaux then stands out with redoubled salience, and the juices of Pessac appear trebled in perfume and vinosity. The appetite is keen and discerning, and the bodily senses remarkably acute, — just as an old Eastern rug, under certain peculiar conditions, may leap into a new maze of unaccustomed hues.

THE PALLIATIVES

THE PALLIATIVES

Is there no hope? the sick man said;
The silent doctor shook his head.
GAY.

HE herculean task undertaken by Count Grammont, to shake off his former charmer, the *rusée* Mlle. Saint Germain, and hoodwink his friend Matta, to placate the wily Marquis de Senantes, and capture the voluptuous Marchioness, was as nought compared to devising a prescription that will effectually propitiate Gout. The *finesse* of the Count, in the end, was equal to the emergency; the physician still remains in fruitless quest.

Of the numerous remedial agents employed to mitigate the pains of the disease, colchicum stands first and foremost, having proved the most efficacious anodyne, not only in the paroxysm, but in numerous stages of numerous forms of the disorder. Its every part and portion is precious, — the corm, the seeds, and the clustered rosy-purple flowers. From time immemorial it has been considered the great antidote to the *materies morbi*, although when taken in considerable quantities, it produces nausea, faintness, and diarrhœa, is injurious to the coating of the stomach, and liable to produce inflammation of the viscera. So, while a powerful, it is none the less a dangerous remedy in injudicious hands, — a fact duly recognised by old Gerarde, who thus refers to it in his *Great Herball* : " The roots of Hermodactyls are of force to purge and are properly given to those that have the Gout. The roots of all the sorts of Mede Saffrons are very hurtful to the stomache."

Precisely how it acts is not known; but that it does act, and sometimes with wondrous efficacy, is beyond contradiction. Still, medical writers, while sanctioning the use of colchicum, yet caution that it be very carefully employed; and of such not a few condemn its use until the attack is well under way; it being thought the sudden checking of an acute attack, or attempting to ward it off through powerful medicines, may defeat the efforts of Nature to eliminate the poison, thus leading to changes in the vessels and internal organs, and inducing the malady to assume the chronic form. " At the commencement of my practice," observes Trousseau, " I attempted to fight with the disease; now I cross my arms and look on; I do nothing, absolutely nothing, to subdue attacks of acute gout."

Iodine, sulphur, arsenic, and mercury have been employed with varying success as alteratives, notably in constitutional Gout and goutiness; and while none of them are specifics for the disease, they have all been found of benefit. In sub-acute and chronic cases, cinchona and its alkaloids have been used with excellent therapeutical results; as also nux vomica and strychnine, due regard being had to individual nervous peculiarities, and to the degree of renal efficiency. Iron has been pronounced one of the most difficult remedies to prescribe with success, its untimely administration almost inevitably deter-mining a fresh paroxysm.

Of other agents employed in combating the dyscrasia, are the salts of lithia, a powerful sol-vent first proposed by Garrod; together with the liberal use of alkalies, the carbonates and com-pounds of potash and soda, with the vegetable acids, lime-water, and magnesia. It is the general opinion that lithia is best when administered in fluid form, or if the tablets be employed, that they be taken with liberal supplies of water, and preferably at least an hour before meals. All these are employed as solvents to induce as far as possible an alkaline condition of the blood, which even in its natural state always contains a certain amount of uric acid.

Large draughts of plain cold water are advised by some as "flushers" to the system. Others recommend various forms of mineral waters, ac-cording to individual cases. These, says Professor Senator, principally tend to remove the various disorders which stand in a more or less close degree of causal relationship to Gout, either as

The Palliatives

antecedents or concomitants. To introduce the desirable quantity of lithia into the system daily, from thirty to forty-five grains of the carbonate should be taken in combination with two to three quarts of water. Garrod specifies guaiacum, a compound made from the resin of Guaiacum officinale or Lignum-vitæ tree of the West Indies, as a remedial agent which he has employed for years to great advantage, both in the cases of old subjects and young patients. Mention is also made by Professor Schultzen of a substance termed sarkosin that is unknown to the pharmacopœia, the difficulty of its preparation and its high price having rendered it thus far prohibitive; this, he asserts, is a marvellous solvent, though he does not state its effect upon the digestion.

Of late years guaiacum has become much better known than formerly, and now takes rank among the most efficacious active remedies in chronic Gout. So highly is it considered by Garrod that, in a paper read before the Royal Medical and Chirurgical Society in May, 1896, he expressed his opinion of its action, based upon a long experience, as follows: —

" 1. Guaiacum is innocuous, and may be taken for an indefinite period of time, and looked upon as a condiment rather than as a drug, — as harmless as ginger or any other condiment.

" 2. Guaiacum possesses a considerable power, but less than colchicum, in directly relieving patients suffering from gouty inflammation of any part; it may be given whenever there is but little fever.

" 3. Guaiacum taken in the intervals of gouty attacks has a considerable power of averting their recurrence; in fact, it is a very powerful prophylactic.

" 4. Guaiacum does not appear to lose its prophylactic power by long-continued use.

" 5. There are a few persons who cannot readily continue the use of guaiacum ; for such cases there are other drugs whose action is in some respects similar as prophylactics ; perhaps serpentary is one of the most powerful of these."

Many of the seventeenth-century herbalists and doctors who have quaffed deeply from the founts

The Palliatives

of Dioscorides and Pliny, are replete with catholicons derived from the vegetable kingdom, such
as all-heal, wood-betony, burdock, gout-wort, hen-
bane, tansy, garden-rue, kidney-wort, May-lily,
great daisy, cowslip, and others too numerous to
mention. Old Gerarde in particular, whom Dib-
din loved to peruse, is always picturesque, whether
speaking of plants or ailments; his allusions to
Gout being of especial vigour and fire.[1]

[1] It (the great-daisie) likewise asswageth the cruel tor-
ment of the gout, used with a few mallows and butter
boiled and made to the forme of a pultis. (*The Herball or
Generall History of Plantes.*)

The Cowslips are recommended against the paine of the
joynts called the Gout, and slackness of the sinews which is
the palsie. (*Ibid.*)

The juice of Onions mixed with the decoction of Penni-
real, and annointed upon the goutie member with a feather,
easeth the same very much. (*Ibid.*)

Corolline or Sea Moss. Dioscorides commendeth it to be
good for the gout which hath need to be cooled. (*Ibid.*)

Figs stamped with the powder of Fenugreeke, and vin-
egar, and applied plaisterwise, doe ease the intollerable paine
of the hot-gout, especially the gout of the feet. (*Ibid.*)

Goutweed or Herb-Gerrard. The very bearing of it
about one easeth paines of the gout, and defends him that

75

Meditations on Gout

Rabelais has Gargantua prescribe a leveret's thigh as excellent for the Gout, — a belief which Pliny also refers to in his *Natural History*. At a later period Huet, referring to the passage of Rabelais, states that even during his day the majority of those afflicted carried the foot of a hare with them as a preventive, — a belief no stranger, perhaps, than the common practice at present of carrying a horse-chestnut in one's

bears it from the disease. — CULPEPPER, *The British Herball and Family Physician.*

Burdock. Tis good for swellings of the spleen, and of all other parts in gouty diseases. — JOHN PECHEY, *The Compleat Herbal of Physical Plants.*

For the Gout, take *Aristolochia rotunda, Althea,* Betony, and the roots of wild Nep, and the roots of the wild Dock cut in pieces after the upper rind is taken away, of each alike quantity, boyl them all in running water till they be soft and thick : then stamp them in a mortar, as small as may be ; and put thereto a little quantity of chimney soot, and a pint of new milk of a Cow, which is all of one intire colour, and as much of the urine of a man that is fasting, and having stirred them all well together, boil them once again on the fire, then as hot as the party can suffer it, apply it to the grieved place, and it will give him ease. GERVAISE MARKHAM, *The English House-Wife.*

The Palliatives

pocket as an antidote for rheumatism, or the faith in the horse-shoe and four-leaved clover.

An old specific, which had descended with some slight variations in its composition from the times of Cælius Aurelianus, was termed Portland Powder, from its having been purchased by the Duke of Portland who distributed the recipe for general use, on account of the service it appeared to have rendered him. Its ingredients, slightly modified from the recipe of the old Greek writers, consist of equal parts of the five following materials, finely powdered and mixed : — birthwort, gentian, germander, ground-pine, and the tops and leaves of the lesser centaury. The dose was a drachm taken fasting every morning for three months; after which it is to be reduced to three quarters of a drachm for three months longer; then to half a drachm for the remainder of the year; after this the same dose is to be continued every other morning only, through the next twelve months, when a cure, it is presumed, will have been accomplished. This was considered by Cullen an extremely dangerous remedy, which, while often lessening the attacks, induced maladies like apoplexy, asthma, or dropsy, that frequently proved fatal. It has also been condemned by various writers.

Another preventive, so far as preventives go, was commended by Dr. Graves, of Dublin, as possessing great virtues, although like the Portland Powder it has fallen into disuse. Its ingredients are as follows: Two ounces of orange-peel; an ounce of powdered rhubarb, and two ounces of the *pulvis aloës cum canellâ* of the Dublin Pharmacopœia, steeped for a week in a quart of brandy. A table-spoonful of the strained infusion is to be taken, mixed with two or three spoonfuls of water, night and morning. Sir Henry Halford has recommended what Dr. Watson considers a better form of prophylactic, viz.: a few grains of rhubarb, with double the quantity of magnesia every day; or some light bitter infusion, with tincture of rhubarb, and about fifteen grains of bicarbonate of potash. Cullen recommended for strengthening the stomach, the use of iron; for supporting its tone, aromatics

The Palliatives

cautiously employed; and when the stomach is liable to indigestion, the use of proper laxatives.

Following the rest of the olden school, Sir William Temple, a martyr by inheritance, presents some strange lenitives for the disease in his quaint and scholarly essay on the subject, to which the sufferer may be referred with entertainment if not with benefit, — the author having died of the affliction, despite his faith at the time in moxa and abstinence. Apart from these specifics, he refers to several cures through the use of guaiacum. One would scarcely care to try the heroic India remedy of burning moxa, a species of moss, over the affected part — even in " long and inveterate gouts; " or the singular sedative of old Prince Maurice of Nassau mentioned in the essay. Neither would one wish to experiment with the method practised by a Lorraine surgeon at the time — of " whipping the naked part with a great rod of nettles till it grew all over blistered." It was the author's firm conviction, nevertheless, that for desperate cases heroic measures are required; and that Gout was

Meditations on Gout

" a companion to be treated like an enemy and by no means like a friend, which grew troublesome chiefly by good usage — that it haunted usually the easy and the rich, the nice and the lazy, who take care to carry it presently to bed and keep it safe and warm ; and indeed lay it up for two or three months, while they give out that it lays up them."[1]

Numerous other remedies or so-termed elixirs —

" Bubbles that glitter as they rise and break — "

have figured since Watson's day. Lartigue's, Blair's, Laville's, and various other specifics are well known ; one of the most recent is that of a chemist to the Duke of Cambridge, who is said to have amassed a large fortune in mending the nobility and patching up the followers of Port. Referring to such forms of medication, Cullen remarks : " I am much disposed to believe the impossibility of a cure of the gout by medicines ; and more certainly still incline to think that whatever may be the possible power of medicines,

[1] *An Essay upon the Cure of the Gout by Moxa* (1677).

yet no medicine for curing the gout has hitherto been found. Although almost every age has presented a new remedy, yet all hitherto offered have very soon been either neglected as useless, or condemned as pernicious." It has furthermore been demonstrated that, even among the accepted medicines, what is useful at one time may prove useless or positively injurious at another. Indeed, with regard to the efficacy of prophylactics, it may be said in the words of the *Fœrie Queene :*

> "No magicks arts hereof had any might,
> Nor bloody words of bold Enchanter's call."

Unquestionably, it is difficult to improve upon the prescription of temperance in diet, and abundant open-air exercise or open-air labour, not only for Gout, but for nearly all forms of stomachic complaints. A sunny temperament also counts for much in exemption from gastric disturbances. One may laugh away indigestion to a great extent, as one may readily goad it on through worry and a sedentary life.

Early rising has repeatedly been included among prophylactics, — a prescription that, seemingly of little value in itself, may be of benefit in a reflex way in that it tends to early retiring; and thus, cutting short conviviality at night, may serve to curtail one's allowance of liquid stimulant.

The value of certain medicinal springs, additionally emphasised by their strict dietary and eliminative treatment, has long been recognized. At the same time their action does not always prove beneficial, and in some instances has resulted most disastrously. It is of the greatest moment, therefore, that the patient be intelligently advised as to the special Spa which will best suit his particular case, constitution, and temperament. Thus to some the Kreutzerbrunnen of Marienbad is recommended; to others the anti-arthritic waters of Kissingen, Wiesbaden, Homburg, or Vichy, according to the particular patient to be prescribed for. And yet so able an authority as Dr. Felix von Niemeyer, professor of pathology at Tübingen, states that he is unable to decide "which of the above springs deserves the preference in the treatment of gout, whether the solution of salt of which the Kissingen and Homburg waters

The Palliatives

consist, removes the plethora more rapidly and completely than Carlsbad and Marienbad water, or the reverse. . . . Nor can we, with our present knowledge, say whether in any particular case the preference should be given to Kissingen, Carlsbad, Wiesbaden, Homburg, or Vichy, and what would constitute the peculiarity of the case which indicates one rather than the others."[1]

This statement, made in 1871, nevertheless does not coincide with the usual experience of experts, who distinctly specify certain Spas for certain conditions and phases of the disorder; Garrod, who has long been recognized as one of the most eminent specialists on the subject, summing up the matter as follows: "The particular water should be selected according to the nature of the case. When the patient is robust and of full habit, the alkaline springs; when torpidity of the bowels predominates, the purgative waters; when there is a want of vascular action, the saline waters; when the skin is inactive, the sulphur waters; lastly, when debility prevails, then the

[1] *Text-Book of Practical Medicine*, vol. ii.

more simple thermal waters should be chosen."
The same writer, referring to hot-air and vapour
baths and other means of increasing the cutaneous secretions, does not hold to the more
or less accepted opinion that excessive perspira-
tion is a means of ridding the system of its
morbid matters.

One hesitates to question so distinguished a
therapeutist as Garrod. Still, so protean is Gout
in its nature and its effects upon different constitutions and temperaments, that it may be
queried whether certain persons may not be
much benefited by the judicious use of the
Turkish bath, as well as by cool baths, and rous-
ing the skin to activity by a vigorous use of the
crash-towel. To some, much walking exercise at
a time when most needed may prove an irritant
to the susceptible joint; while horseback exercise
is not within the reach of all, or for various reasons may not always be advisable. Moreover,
with some whose excreting powers through the
skin are lethargic, and even with many in whom
this function is normal, the quick cold or cool

The Palliatives

bath, taken when the body is warm, exercises a most tonical and invigorating influence upon the general system.

These are considerations, like numerous others with reference to foods, stimulants, and various forms of exercise, that may not be regulated by any universal rule ; but rather by the age, and peculiar conditions governing each individual. To supplement Garrod's and Niemeyer's statements concerning mineral springs, not a few physicians rigidly proscribe the waters of Carlsbad, Vichy, Vals, and some others, as dangerous. Trousseau, the French authority, believes in the beneficial action of medicinal springs ; but in a degree which is very limited. Not a year passes, he declares, in which he does not see the evil consequences of the use of mineral waters in Gout.

Diet and exercise, however, are the most favoured catholicons, despite the fact that in attempting to trace the operative effects of certain foods and drinks in creating and fostering the malady, there exist many subtleties which have baffled the physician. The hypothesis has been advanced, that dietary articles containing a considerable amount of saline principles, such as salts of potash, tend to promote the activity of the secreting organs, more particularly the function of the kidneys; while many such substances, even if acid to the stomach, yet tend to alkalise the blood and animal fluid from the decomposition of the vegetable acid and a formation of the carbonate of the alkali. It is thus that lemon juice is said to be beneficial in rheumatism, consisting as it does largely of pure citric acid with a little lime and potash, — the presence of these latter as alkalies being supposed to act favourably in neutralising the rheumatic poison.

THE REGIMEN

THE REGIMEN

EVEN of more importance than
what is eaten, is what is
drunk; and observation shows
that it is not distilled spirits,
but the stronger wines and
malt-liquors which favour the
production of the disorder.[1] "We should write
few prescriptions," observes Niemeyer, "but
should regulate the habits of the patient." "Live
on sixpence a day, and earn it," was Sir John
Abernethy's well-known reply to the question,
"What is the cure for the Gout?" — a remedy
that would apply, no doubt, to many other afflictions as well. But like Æsop's fable of the cat
and the mice, the remedy is even worse than the

[1] Dr. F. W. Pavy, *A Treatise on Food and Dietetics.*

89

emergency; and who is there possessed of sufficient resolution to attach the bell?

If the stomach could only speak from its innermost caverns, voicing what it craved and what it resented, there would be far easier sailing. But it is almost impossible to constantly stroke it the right way. The innocent-looking orange that forms the stepping-stone to your breakfast, the grape-fruit that has been pronounced an antidote to rheumatism, or the strawberries that are deemed so healthful, may each and all be breeders of discord and fermentation in disguise. In the natural course of satisfying its needs, so many forms of aliments are partaken of that it becomes all the more difficult to decide which are the chief offenders. To go through a course of experiment with a certain order of flesh, starch, and vegetable foods with a view of tracing out the culprits, were a tedious and difficult proceeding. The problem then would be to detect the chief offender, where each one would lay the blame upon the others, and unite in the chorus, "Stop thief!"

The Regimen

And inasmuch as fats, starch, and albuminoids have each their separate processes of digestion, and severally and conjointly claim attention as regards their influence in the modifications of nutrition, as also in any remedial measures that may be adopted towards comparatively permanent relief — the complexity of the situation becomes trebly apparent.

How is one to know, withal, whether the sweets or the sours are at the bottom of the trouble, or if both are equally prolific of mischief ? Experimenting with sweets might at once arouse the enemy ; while trifling with salads and acid articles might cause him to whet his tushes for a fresh attack.

As regards wines, the quandary is still worse, when one considers the various effects of the same wines upon various persons, and even upon the same persons at various times. Or, as Master Burton has anatomically phrased it, " So one thing may be good and bad to several parties, upon divers occasions ; and that which is conducing to one man, in one case, the same time is opposite in another."

Meditations on Gout

On the other hand, any endeavours to regulate oneself by the physicians, when stomachs are so radically different in their special likes and dislikes, is equally out of the question. The further difficulty of pleasing one's stomach also occurs in the natural course of events, inasmuch as certain foods are placed upon the table, and one must perforce choose from these. And of such, which are innocuous and which are noxious becomes a matter most difficult to determine; when even the use of oat-meal has been known to be a prolific source of trouble, and the free use of celery, both in cooked and uncooked form, has been deemed of much benefit in not a few instances. Oat-meal, it may be remarked, often proves very heating to many, and is a not infrequent cause of stomachic derangements both in children and adults; the large amount of gluten it contains rendering it difficult of digestion. Many of the tough, leathery gelatine compounds which are often placed on the table by an incompetent priestess of the range, are likewise, in many stomachs, rocks of stumbling to digestion.

The Regimen

To what extent, furthermore, when acquired
and not transmitted, depending as it does upon
so many stomachic aberrations and vagaries,
even unto slight gastric derangements on the
start — to what extent may not Gout in numerous instances be largely a case of predisposition,
just as one may have a susceptibility for catching
cold, or a talent for business or money-getting?
Cullen, however, has already anticipated the
reply to the question: "In a disease depending
so much upon a predisposition, the assigning
occasional causes must be uncertain; as in the
predisposed, the occasional causes may not
always appear, and in persons not predisposed,
they may appear without effect."

What, then, by way of pacifying the stomach,
shall the afflicted eat and drink, and wherewithal
shall they be regulated? To one possessed of a
full appetite — and very many who are subject to
gastric disorders are possessed of good appetites —
it is as easy to render life a burden by constant
restrictions as it is to render living onerous by
flagrant excess and gross violation of self-evident

hygienic rules. The man who abjures all alcoholic fluids, as compared with him who partakes of them in moderation, may or may not add a year or two to his life; but he foregoes a source of lightening care and lessening the asperities of daily existence. Of course for those who cannot preserve the golden mean and are incapable of using without abusing, the only remedy is total abstention from alcohol, and a strict set of rules to apply to all forms of nourishment. For not only wine, but many other things as well are —

" — like rain, which when falling on mire makes it the
    fouler;
But when it strikes the good soil wakes it to beauty and
    bloom."

But it is far from following that he who renounces all spirituous beverages, or gives himself up to stomachic monasticism, will thereby necessarily escape the bane of dyspepsia or rheumatism, even though he may run the gantlope of Gout in comparative safety. Nor for the cure of a purely acute malady — especially if induced by causes of an exasperating temporary nature, when

The Regimen

severe dietary restrictions become imperative — is it always necessary or advisable to continue an ascetic treatment. But a peculiarity of Gout is that it seldom occurs without repeating itself in the acute stage, or merging into some of its protean phases.

The question of foods and fluids becomes accordingly of notable consequence in connection with Gout. What is one to resign, therefore, and what is one to retain amid the innumerable aliments contributed by the storehouse of the earth for the maintenance and delectation of mankind ?

In the varied advice that is proffered by medical writers respecting regimen in the disease, there are many opposing theories, founded as they are upon the various theories of the nature of the malady. " The whole point of the diet treatment of uric-acid disease," in the opinion of Haig, " is to cut out the butcher, and live by the baker, the dairyman, and the fruiterer."[1] A milk diet has frequently been found

[1] Dr. Alexander Haig, *Uric Acid as a Factor in the Causation of Disease.*

advantageous so long as it is persisted in, but when discontinued it is considered to result unfavourably in rendering the patient still more susceptible to toxic alterations. Vegetarianism is commended by some, although this is disapproved by such authorities as Gairdner, Scudamore, Garrod, Lecorché, and numerous others. A mixed and varied diet, on the other hand, with a moderate supply of meat, and due restriction in the use of acids and acid-producing elements, as opposed to a strictly vegetarian or other regimen, is considered the best suited for general application. In other words, such substances, whether solids or fluids, as are most easily digested and are least liable to mal-assimilation, should be chosen. Proper cooking will have much to do with remedial measures; a bad cook can ruin the best digestion, as good cookery can do much towards regulating the well-being of the internal functions. Upon this perplexing subject — the relation of foods and drinks to the disease — we again find Professor Senator a sapient counsellor : —

The Regimen

"Roughly speaking, the diet should be vegetable rather than animal, but absence from meat should not be pushed so far as strict vegetarianism. A mixed diet is accordingly the best — a diet containing a minimum of fatty matter, and in which the proportion of albuminoids, especially of meat, is regulated in each individual case with due regard to constitutional strength, digestive power, occupation, etc. As a general rule gouty persons should only eat meat once a day, at their chief meal. Smoked and salt meat and fish, pork, cheese, farinaceous compounds containing much oily matter and highly spiced — indeed all culinary delicacies should be absolutely forbidden. Eggs and dishes containing them should be avoided as much as possible. On the other hand all kinds of soup, the more delicate varieties of meat, fish, shell-fish (oysters) in moderation, fresh vegetables and fruit may be recommended. Tea and coffee should be altogether abjured, or when the patient cannot bring himself to do this, should be taken very weak. The patient's drink at meal times should be water, —

either plain water or one of the natural or artificial carbonated waters containing alkalies or
alkaline chlorides (soda-water, seltzer, Faching,
Bilin, Giesshuebler Sauerbrunnen, carbonate of
lithia, etc. Alcoholic liquors should never be
taken to quench thirst, but only as roborants
when they are really needed; the best form then
is a good red wine, neat, or diluted with water,
or else a light beer brewed with a small proportion of hops; the fiery southern wines, and those
which are acidulous, champagne, and heavy beer
(porter, etc.) must be forbidden."

It will be perceived from the foregoing advice
that the sufferer, in order to free himself from
repeated onslaughts on the part of the enemy,
must govern his palate with an iron hand, and
enter into a solemn compact with that functionary to relinquish all serious flirting with the
sirens of the kitchen and the *houris* of the wine-
cellar. The stomach, above all things, must be
propitiated, and its good graces obtained as nearly
as may be. To be sure, the price is an expensive
one, calling as it does for the renunciation of

The Regimen

accustomed gustatory delights which have become a second nature to the individual. The philosophically inclined may reason with justice that few things that are really worth having can be obtained without certain sacrifices, — usually of labour or pains of some kind, the expenditure of money, or both. In the case of Gout there is this advantage, — that one's wine-bills may be lowered, and even the cards of compliment of the market-man and grocer may come in for their share of curtailment. And the wise may also justly reason that habit is a tyrant whose thrall has nothing in common with true enjoyment and is inimical to true happiness. The vegetarian who has renounced the flesh-pots, becomes not only content with his lot, but enjoys it, or affects to enjoy it; while the teetotaler, freed from the trammels of choosing among a multiplicity of vintages, waxes fairly riotous in the praise of his chosen beverage. Yet appetite too often rules, and fasting is proverbially hard. The fact remains that there is more pleasure in fondling with the minor vices than in courting the virtues, especially in peccadilloes of eating and drinking; and the seductive call of the palate is always far easier to obey than the duty-call of the stomach. It is easy enough to abstain when severe affliction comes, and still easier to relapse into one's accustomed ways when the crisis has passed, —

> " The devil was sick, the devil a monk would be;
> The devil was well, the devil a monk was he."

Regiminal precautions of a similar nature to those of Professor Senator are generally advised by the profession, with variations governed by the special case under consideration. For those variable elements, individuality and temperament, differing so widely as they do in man, must always enter into consideration in remedial measures. The physician should study his patient's constitution, as the agriculturist requires to familiarise himself with the soils he cultivates where certain elements may be lacking or certain noxious weeds are prone to appear.

The prominent causative factor in Gout being acidity, which induces a corresponding decrease

The Regimen

of the normal alkalinity of the blood, it would seem to be of paramount importance that the patient avoid such foods and drinks as are known to provoke acidity, whether such foods and drinks be primarily of a highly acidulous nature, or whether they are merely acid-provoking agents. Yet it is well known that acids and acid-producing aliments may be taken by some patients with much more impunity than others, dependent not only upon the individual, but also upon climate, season, and mode of life which may operate as mitigating or influencing factors. So that sub-acid fruits, salads, and even wine in moderation may prove much less harmful in many cases than others; though it should not be forgotten that wine and beer require to be partaken of with extreme discretion. In all such instances the subject who has attentively studied his own constitution and digestion, should be fully as competent to judge as the physician. In this connection — the affinity that diet holds to acidity and acidity to Gout — the observations of Ewart, who has made a close study of the theme in his treatise of nearly six hundred pages, are of particular interest, more especially as illustrative of the idiosyncrasies of the disease:

" Looking back into the clinical history of the subjects who acquire gout through high living, we often fail to trace any previous tendency to acidity. They are usually endowed with an originally strong digestion which only gives way at the approach of the gouty stage. Moreover, extreme acidity is presented by many subjects who do not develop the slightest tendency to gout. The mode of origin of acquired gout in itself suggests the operation of some nutritional disorder, whilst the result of this nutritional defect is obvious in the eventual relative atrophy of the tissue elements.

" It is conceivable that, as suggested by Beneke, the undue acidity may be itself the by-product of the faulty metamorphosis of cells. This would explain its persistence in inherited goutiness, even when metabolism is no longer oppressed and depressed by a reckless excess of ingesta. According to this view, a depressed and faulty metabolism

would be the first departure, and abnormal secretion would be its outcome. . . . Meanwhile clinical analysis has made it clear that both in gout
and in goutiness there are numerous varieties,
and that, indeed, no two cases are absolutely alike.
Two practical principles are its direct outcome:
' Each patient has an individual gout of his own,
for which an individual treatment has to be de-
vised; ' and, above all, ' We should treat the
patient rather than the disease.' "

Are fruits instrumental as acid-promoters, and
thereby in inducing Gout and gastric disorders ?
On this question, widely different opinions pre-
vail, some deeming all fruit injurious, others considering only certain kinds disadvantageous, and
still others regarding nearly all forms as a direct
corrective. By Linnæus the strawberry was held
to be antagonistic to Gout, although generally
found to be difficult of digestion. Garrod dis-
approves of all stone fruits, and of apples and
pears unless baked; but recommends strawberries
in small quantities, oranges, grapes, and other suc-
culent species. Grapes and oranges, which easily

yield their juice without any of the indigestible substance being swallowed, are pronounced by Ewing to be of all fruit the most suitable.

Following in the lines of Crato of old, who regarded nearly all fruits as injurious to the stomach, and Villanovanus, who held that they infected the blood and should be very sparingly used, Hoy, in his convenient treatise, " Eating and Drinking," has discussed this topic at greater length and precision than most modern writers on the subject. With many of his conclusions, one may or may not agree, although he declares that his experience is founded on careful experiments and observation dating from thirty years. This experience leads him to the belief that the majority of varieties and species of cultivated sub-acid fruits are distinctly pernicious to the majority of persons, both young and old — a prime cause of indigestion and very numerous disorders of the blood. Sweet fruits, like the fig, banana, and date, as also the pineapple, he commends, as they are merely wild fruits, and have not been changed from their natural conditions or flavour by man. On the other hand, the fruits condemned by him, he states, are forced or abnormal variations, as is shown when cultivated, and afterward allowed to run wild; then they immediately retrograde, and assume the sour and inedible qualities originally inherent in them. By assiduous cultivation under artificial conditions, man has modified the progenitors of our present domestic fruits; he has made them acceptable to the palate, but he has not eliminated their harmful qualities.

Not only the strawberry, currant, and raspberry, but equally the apple, pear, cherry, peach, and grape are placed under ban, while hyper-acid species like the grape-fruit, shaddock, and orange are pronounced still more active agents of stomachic fermentation, all tending to diminish the alkalinity of the blood. "The grape-fruit," sa_s the author, "having in its composition a large percentage of free acid and a somewhat bitter taste, is a favourite morning stimulant for those whose appetite needs forcing. It is known in Europe as the 'forbidden fruit,' and many would be wise if they would so regard it." "Every cemetery in the land," he continues, "contains many little monuments on which the inscription should be, 'Killed by eating fruits under the erroneous opinion that they formed a necessary part of infant diet.'" The acid fruits, he holds, are not adapted to furnish nutriment to man; and tend to rob the blood of its alkaline principle — a consequent he applies in a lesser degree to the sub-acid species when partaken of in a raw state, as also to many of these when partaken of in the form of jellies and preserves. With certain meats, however, experience has shown that sub-acid fruits are wisely eaten, as apple-sauce with roast-goose and duck, cranberries with turkey, and fried apples with roast pork. In view of the theory advanced and discoursed upon at length by the author, it may perhaps be possible to trace the as yet undiscovered baneful principle of wine as a promoter of Gout; and to assign its poisonous element in the disease, not to the alcohol it contains, but to the essence of the fruit which lends to wine its exquisite savour and perfume.

The Regimen

Concerning the nature of cultivated fruits in promoting acidity and fermentation, it may be observed that varieties vary largely in their digestive and non-digestive properties. Broadly speaking, crisp and firm fruits are not as readily digested as those of an opposite character. A Fameuse or a Jonathan apple is one thing; a Gravenstein or a Greening another, — the latter varieties being much more acidulous, and being more apt to disagree with some. So also with the Alpine and Hautbois strawberries, or our own wild strawberry, as compared to the unripened cone of the Sharpless, the intensely sour Wilson, and numerous highly acetous kinds. Of the qualities of the Spitzenberg apple, it is unnecessary to speak, while of the Northern Spy it may be said that although somewhat tart, it possesses an especially refreshing and pleasant acid. The excessively sugary varieties of plums, like many of the Gages, and pears, such as the honied Seckel and Sheldon, are liable to provoke acidity from their over-sweetness. The silica or gritty particles in certain varieties of pears, similar to some of the many-seeded small fruits, like the raspberry and blackberry, often proves a source of indigestion. But who shall say that the ambrosia of a well-ripened Morris White peach and attar-of-rose savour of an Urbaniste or a Josephine pear should be left for the wasp and robin to extract upon the tree, and not be worthy to add their flavour to the dinner-table during the wintry season !

There is an appointed time to eat fruits, a period of maturity when the fruit is in entire possession of its virtues, which is little understood. The peach, plum, apricot, nectarine, and grape are best fresh from the tree and the vine. The apple and pear, notably the pear, should be plucked before they are fully ripe, and allowed to mellow, like wine. Some varieties mature early, some much more slowly. Many fruits are highly indigestible until kept for a considerable period. Others, that are digestible when ripe upon the bough, like the peach, are often picked when under-ripe for the market, and hence are received by the consumer in an improper condition.

The Regimen

In many English estates where the peach and nectarine are grown under glass, it is customary to suspend a net beneath the trees, such fruit only being gathered as falls of its own accord. As an instance of the difference between well-matured and immature fruit, one has but to compare a Russet apple in its leathery stage when recently plucked, to a specimen of the same variety that has been allowed to fully mature; or an Anjou pear tasted in October with one which has been stored and permitted to develop its vinous juices. But fancy a garden stripped of its fruit-trees, and a farm despoiled of its orchards! To accept Hoy's theory in its almost unconditional exclusion were to banish one of the noblest of the agricultural arts, and lay waste the teeming plantations of Pomona that so generously contribute to the resources of the husbandman and the nourishment of mankind.

Placing the doctors and professional dietetists aside, the taste has its longings which it is sometimes well to heed, general opinion to the contrary notwithstanding. If its fancies are often adverse to the true welfare of the stomach, and it prove itself frequently an unreliable Cerberus in guarding that important organ from its assailants, — its promptings, on the contrary, are not infrequently a demand from the seat of internal weal or woe for the exact panacea that will best meet its especial requirements at such especial time. The palate therefore, prompted by the stomach, has its likes and dislikes, its hankerings and aversions which, even where these are apparently anomalous, it is often wise to heed; for *toujours perdrix* in the matter of a set line of food and drink may even decide the Gout to show his fangs anew, and cry out for variety and relief. By this statement it will not be understood that it is advisable for those who may be suffering from chronic Gout to indulge in Port and red currants, or for a diabetes patient to assuage his thirst with Champagne.

There are times, however, when sweets or acids, as the case may be, are intensely craved, much as animals crave salt ; and the question then arises by those who do not practise making a daily diary of

The Regimen

their stomachs, whether these should be entirely abjured. " Good is a good doctor, but Bad is sometimes a better," Emerson truly says. Many a man can ascribe his convalescence from a fit of sickness to a salad, a fruit, or a glass of wine which his physician would not have countenanced at the time, just as Count Béchamel dated his recovery and fifteen years of added life to three glasses of old Constance and a Périgord *pâté* at a time when he had been given up to die. In the instance of fruit, like many other kinds of aliments, experience should be the best teacher, and the demands and aversions of one's particular constitution, as opposed to mere dogma, should be the safest guide. To be constantly theorising of what one may eat and what one should leave alone, or considering whether one should gra-hamise or vegetarianise — measuring this and weighing that — is enough in itself to develop gastralgia, and render existence a torture.

Finally, as concerns the choice of foods in Gout, a case mentioned by Cheyne, one of the old masters, is worthy of citation. For, however the medical profession of the present day may cavil at his theory, the patient will doubtless find much to commend in the "triming" method he advances, and in his daily allowance of a pint of " some generous, soft, balsamick Wine."

" A Gentleman of fine Parts, grieviously afflicted with the *Gout*, and with a perpetual *Lowness*, *Sinking*, and *Oppression*, both in *Fits*, and the *Intervals*, being weary of a life under such Miseries, was willing to attempt anything probable to mitigate them. But being justly afraid of a *total Milk and Vegetable Diet* . . . ; therefore a *triming* and middling Diet being propos'd, chiefly of light, fresh River Fish (as least inflaming, and not over enriching the Juices) alternately with Milk and Vegetables; and every Day the Value of a *Pint* of some generous, soft, balsamick Wine (as *Sack*, *Canary*, or *Palm*), he readily and cheerfully enter'd upon it. This *Method* abated both the *Violence, Duration,* and Frequency of his Fits in a few Years, without any Danger at all; especially by almost every Night taking a few Spoonfuls of a *Rhubarb* and *Bark*

Bitter, made on Wine with Aromaticks, in the Intervals; and he has now only a very tolerable, short, regular Fit once a Year, and soon gets about his Business again, and is in likelihood to go on with Health and Strength to a great Age.

"I cannot omit here to observe, that if any person designs, either for the sake of *Health*, *Long Life,* or Freedom from Diseases, to regulate his Diet, I universally prefer to all others this *triming* Method of an *alternate* Diet of *Milk* and *Vegetables* one Day, and the other plain or young *Animal* Food, and a moderate portion of *Wine ;* for if his Case requires his descending still lower, yet this *triming Diet* will be the best and safest first step to begin with; and if his Recovery thereafter be so perfect, that he may rise to a higher Diet, this will make the *Transition* safer; and even those who love palatable and delicious Foods, to a great degree, will bear a *Maigre* Day more easily when they know they shall have a *Gaudy* one the next; and I have known those, who from a weak *Nervous* and *Cachectick* Habit

Meditations on Gout

have arriv'd to a confirm'd State of Health, noble Spirits, and great Age, by this *Trick* alone; so that Fasting and Abstinence in this manner might seem not more a *religious* than it ought to be reckon'd a *medical* Institution." [1]

After all has been said by doctors, dietarians, and philosophers the question of diet and the golden rules of hygiene have nowhere been more plainly set forth than by the son of Sirach of old : —

"Take not thy pleasure in much good cheer. . . .
Be not unsatiable in any dainty thing, nor too greedy upon meats.
For excess of meats bringeth sickness, and surfeiting will turn into choler.
By surfeiting have many perished; but he that taketh heed prolongeth his life. . . .
Shew not thy valiantness in wine. . . .
For all things are not profitable to all men, neither hath every soul pleasure in everything." [2]

[1] George Cheyne, M. D. *The English Malady: Or A Treatise of Nervous Diseases of all kinds.* (2d ed., 1734.)
[2] *Ecclesiasticus*, 18, 37, 31, 37.

THE PROSCRIBED FLUIDS

THE PROSCRIBED GUIDE

THE PROSCRIBED FLUIDS

If your Physitian thinke it not good that you drinke wine,
or eate such and such meates Care you not for that, I will
finde you another that shall not be of his opinion.

MONTAIGNE.

Nous sommes gens qui n'avons pas
Toutes nos aises ici-bas.

LA FONTAINE.

GREATER discrimination, as
has already been observed, ob-
tains with reference to wines
and alcoholic drinks than with
respect to foods ; the consideration of this feature being of
notable interest and presenting many anomalies.
Alcohol is almost universally considered injurious
in the diathesis, both by increasing the production
of uric acid, and by lessening the excretory power
of the kidneys through its continued use. Yet
this subject is a relative one, depending in no little
measure upon the quantity consumed and the
form of fluid in which it is combined. The

Meditations on Gout

medical opinion, nevertheless, regarding *certain* wines and liquors is almost unanimous. In the *codex expurgatorius* are included such wines as are rich in alcohol and saccharine matter, or of a heating, stimulating nature; those which are generally considered most baneful being Port, Madeira, Burgundy, Sherry, Malaga, Champagne, the heavy growths of the Côtes du Rhône and the honied products of the Pyrénées Orientales.[1] To such must be added the luscious sweet Sauternes. These with their engaging colour, fragrance, savour, and sparkle, as they gleam or foam in the glass and distil their generous warmth, are to be shunned as one would the noisome effluvium of the Upas tree. Their rubies are tainted, and their ambers infect.

Malt liquors are also usually proscribed, notably porter and heavy ales. As far back as Galen's day, fermented cider was thought to have little power in inducing the disease, whereas when taken in considerable quantities in its sweet and partially fermented state, it is recognised as a

[1] Nothing is more potent than port wine in leading to the production of gout. — DR. F. W. PAVY.

The Proscribed Fluids

predisposing cause. In those districts where it is largely consumed, Gout is little known; and hence it has been regarded by many persons as a preventive; the fact being lost sight of that it is thus largely employed by those who lead a simple and laborious life, and earn their daily bread by the sweat of their brow. Were the Normandy, Brittany, or the Devonshire peasant to inherit a generous fortune early in life, and, lapsing into luxury, continue his copious libations of apple-juice to wash down rich *entrées* whilst leading a sedentary and irregular existence, it is a question whether cider would not prove a dangerous draught.

Distilled spirits are regarded as considerably less injurious than those forms of beverage already specified. The same applies to the lighter kinds of French and German wines, and the lighter beers as brewed in Germany, — German beer as made for export being considerably stronger than that brewed for home consumption, and losing in sprightliness and delicacy when subject to long voyages. Of distilled liquors, rum is considered the most objectionable except arrack, absinthe, or any liquor distilled from rice; or liquors like the sweet cordials in which the essential oils of various aromatic herbs, and extraneous sugar are employed. Garrod recommends French brandy as the beverage most suitable for those of a strongly marked diathesis, to be taken in very limited quantities, freely diluted with water.

Why distilled spirits should be less pernicious than fermented beverages, has not been determined; the sages simply do not know. Again, how far alcoholic fluids are pernicious in themselves, or how far a united action of alcohol and food is responsible for detrimental chemical changes in such food has not been defined. It is not the relatively small amount of alcohol that enters into the composition of many wines which works the mischief, it would appear, so much as its combination with their other ingredients; or, as previously mentioned, its evil fusion with numerous aliments. Certain it is, from abundant testimony which cannot be disputed, that wine, more noticeably sweet and heavy wines, does exert a pronounced influence in developing the dyscrasia; and that sugar, as also saccharine, is more difficult to digest in connection with wine than in any other form.

All wines that contain much tannin are considered prejudicial; while those which cause a marked diuretic action are pronounced less capable of aggravating the malady. Notwithstanding this, the wines of Bordeaux, or so-termed "clarets," are generally recommended, where the use of wine is countenanced. And yet the Bordeaux wines, especially those growths of good years,—so dear to the wine-lover,—are rich in tannin, a component that bends greatly to their quality and their preservation.

"Neither the acid, sugar, nor any known principle contained in these liquors," says Garrod, "can as yet be proved to impart to the alcohol its predisposing influence; for wines the least acid and liquors the least sweet, are found among the most baneful. Alcoholic fluids which have little tendency to cause dyspepsia, and those which more especially act as diuretics, can, as far as gout is concerned, be taken with greater impunity than beverages of an opposite character." " If you drink wine, you have the gout, and if you do not drink wine the gout will have you," is an old saying. " Water alone is bad and dangerous," was a precept of Sydenham, who recommended the use of a mild ale brewed in London, and permitted the use of wine, — the wines of Spain and the Canaries in preference to those of France and Germany. With the changes in vinification since the seventeenth century, however, it is highly improbable that such would have been his advice at the present time. " Wine may prove injurious as an ordinary beverage," according to Trousseau, " but the exclusive use of water will be still more hurtful."[1]

Among the Spanish wines and growths of Andalusia, that of Manzanilla or Mançanilla, made near Xeres, is the driest and most aromatic, acting upon many constitutions as a stomachic

---

[1] It is hurtful to drink wine or water alone, and wine mingled with water is pleasant and delighteth the taste. (*Apocrypha*, 2 *Maccabees* xv. 39.)

and diuretic. Sherry in general is not open to the great objection of Port, inasmuch as but a very small quantity of foreign alcohol is added to it, — usually at the most a few bottles of brandy to each butt; in the brown sherries, an addition of boiled wine is made to impart the desired dark shade. Madeiras, on their part, vary largely in qualities, — some being over-sweet through the fermentation having been checked, and the addition of brandy to the must; others being astringent; and all receiving an admixture of brandy in a greater or less degree on exportation.

In the case of the sweet Sauternes, this excessive sweetness is produced not only by the selection and crushing of such grapes as have ripened to a point of over-ripeness, but by arresting the fermentation of the must through sulphuring. This arrest of the fermentation also prevails in many of the finer *Auslesen* of the Rheingau and the Bavarian Palatinate, to the injury of the keeping qualities and the finer vinous properties of the wines.

Meditations on Gout

Generally speaking, the lighter wines of France and Germany, as made to-day, are a refreshing, tonical, and pleasing beverage; and in many countries the daily use of such wines appears to be distinctly favourable to the general health. Recent statistics of the different departments of France, whose wines vary widely in character, show that the department of the Gironde, one of the greatest producing and consuming districts of that country, as well as the department of the Yonne, are especially noticeable for the longevity of their inhabitants. In both of these departments red and white wines are generously consumed; the red predominating in the Gironde, while in the Yonne, the home of Chablis, much more white wine is drunk than in the districts about Bordeaux.

Some subtle and deleterious property, notwithstanding, — a property that proves deleterious at least to certain constitutions, and that is more peculiar to fruits than to other forms of vegetable growths like cereals, — it would seem, lurks in the fermented fruit of the vine, such property being much less marked in brandy, the distilled product of the *Folle Blanche* grape. Some constituent of the grape itself, similar to the toxic component of the strawberry and certain other fruits — more highly emphasised in red varieties of the grape than in white, unless the rich saccharine white wines be included, and yet more pronounced when the grapes are fermented on the skin — undoubtedly constitutes the baneful element. Does this toxic ingredient reside in some volatile oil or œnanthic ether of the skin of certain grapes ; is it evolved in the fusion of the particular fruit essences with the alcohol engendered by fermentation; or is it the pernicious combination of wine with certain articles of food that is at fault and to which the formation of the poisonous elements in digestion, as far as wine is responsible, should be ascribed ?   These are questions that as yet await the answer of the analyst.

In the instance of malt-liquors, the solution is more readily definable.   It is recognised that any ingredients employed to take the place of hops and barley-malt, or to assist in quick development, clarification, or a frothy head, however cunningly employed to deceive the taste, are injurious, and frequently responsible for dangerous kidney and liver affections. Even in distilled liquors it is well known that rice is a detrimental component, and that it becomes still more hurtful in fermented fluids. Long experience has demonstrated that the light beers of Germany when drunk in that country, as compared with the malted products of other countries, are relatively harmless unless drunk in inordinate quantities; that the heavy English ales and porters are objectionable as a daily beverage ; and that the consumption of all adulterated forms of beer and ale is attended with peril. It may be said with reference to the comparative noxiousness or innocuousness of malt liquors that the following conditions play the principal part : the use of hops and barley-malt alone, the quality and quantity of the hops and malt employed, the purity of the water, the system of fermentation, the proper maturity of the fluid, and the presence or absence of aldehyde, gluten of the malt, and

The Proscribed Fluids

fusel oil. All these are important mediums with relation to the injurious or non-injurious effects of beer and ale.

With wine, as has been stated, the problem is far more difficult to determine. What, then, are the constituent parts of wine; what elements has it extracted from the soil, the sun, the dew, the rain, the atmosphere, and the vat; what does its fluid resolve itself into in the retort of the chemist? Of what are they composed — these ethers, odours, and fugacious fragrances and flavours that have hived and ripened their delicious sweetnesses in the bottle through the long autumns and winters, and swift-speeding springs and summers of the years?

The components of the product of the vine consist principally of water and alcohol, — the quantity of spirit which is evolved by the fermentation of the saccharine matter in the vat varying according to the seasons, the locality, the kinds of grapes employed, and the period and mode of gathering the fruit. Besides this water and alcohol, there are contained numerous soluble ingredients, as œnanthic and other ethers, free acids, and salts, together with extractive or mucilaginous or colouring matters, and astringent and saccharine properties. The acids and salts are composed principally of the acid tartrate of potash, and different forms of tartaric acid, much of which is decomposed during fermentation, as also, in the generality of wines, malic, citric, and acetic acids. There exist, likewise, relatively small amounts of other salts, such as iron, magnesia, and phosphate of lime. It may be briefly said that the distinguishing characteristics of wines lie first of all in the species of fruit from which they are made,—the different qualities of the growths of a district varying according to the soil, location, and aspect of the territory on which the vine is grown. These distinctive bouquets, flavours, and alcoholic strengths become marked still further, even in adjoining vineyards, by the special combinations of grapes that form the must, and different methods of vitification and vinification. Moreover, the savour, as well as the proportions of the chemical constituents, of wine are largely dependent upon the mood of the season — whether Favonius smiles, or Vertumnus frowns ; whether the year prove hot or cold, moist or dry, tardive or precocious.

It is claimed from statistics that Rhine and Mosel wines are the most harmless. Dr. Goeris, writing from Mayence, where the adult man drinks on an average three hundred and sixty bottles yearly, many drinking very much more, states that during twenty years only four cases of Gout came under his observation, and these were persons who led a sedentary life, and were addicted to the pleasures of the table, confining themselves by no means to the use of Rhenish wines. In Bingen, the very heart of the Rheingau, Gout, he says, is almost unknown. From these facts he concludes that Rhine wines contain no properties productive of the disorder, which is produced by admitting into the system an immoderate quantity of azotic nourishment; together with insufficient secretion and respiration, as also lack of exercise. On the contrary, Gout is of common occurrence in Munich and numerous places where beer is drunk in very large quantities; while adulterated beers, or beer in which glucose and other sophistications form a part, are undoubtedly as pernicious in their effects as Port.

With respect to the influence of the wines of Bordeaux, a resident writes: " It is a mistake to suppose that these are a cause of gout. Our medical men prescribe them for those whose blood is poor, and who require strengthening. Certainly, if too much is taken, it will do harm, as too much food will; but it is otherwise considered beneficial for the health of every one to drink true Bordeaux wine."

An English gentleman, replying to the inquiry which wine he found most likely to bring on Gout, states that in his instance the disease is hereditary, his father and two brothers having died from it. In his case he has observed that it is never developed except through indigestion, and hence his self-treatment has been to anticipate indigestion, rather than to cure it. Though he has found its occurrence depends upon a multitude of circumstances very different from the taking of wine, he also finds that certain wines are much more likely to produce it than others ; and these, therefore, he avoids. The two which he is obliged to be most cautious about are Port and Burgundy. All others he takes freely without any reason to believe them at all injurious; even Burgundy and Port he can take, in moderation, with perfect impunity. "Ten or fifteen years ago," he continues, "before I understood how to manage myself so well as I have since learned by experience to do, I used to have gout three or four times a year. I then adopted my present precautionary system, including great moderation in Port, and taking principally white wines, and I found immediate benefit. For the last ten years my principal wine daily is fine Madeira, and frequently Champagne ; and my attacks have been reduced from three in twelve months to four in twelve years ! You will observe that I condemn no wine in moderation ; but those I find least likely to cause indigestion, and consequently the best to avoid gout, are Champagne and Madeira; that is, assuming both to be fine wine, pure, and of the best quality; but the grand prophylactic is, not merely to keep down indigestion, but to forestall and prevent its approach."[1]

"I call my gout," Lowell declares, on the other hand, "the unearned increment from my good grandfather's Madeira, and think how excellent it must have been, and sip it cool from the bin of fancy, and wish he had left me the cause instead of the effect."

It will be noticed that in the instance previously cited, Madeira and Champagne, two wines that are invariably placed upon the black-list, were drunk with comparative impunity. This would point to one of two conclusions: either that Champagne and Madeira are healthful anti-arthritic beverages to some, — the former, when not sweet, or adulterated with alum as it frequently is in the "brut" form, acting perhaps as a

---

[1] Thomas George Shaw, *Wine, the Vine, and the Cellar.*

The Proscribed Fluids

tonic, and the latter as a diuretic, — or that so far as wines and foods go, there can be no certain regimen prescribed which will meet the infinite vagaries of the universal stomach.

This interesting experience, however, comes nearer to a remedy than any contained in medical treatises, without abstinence from alcoholic beverages and semi-starvation as the penalty. But as the experience stands, it is of little avail, through default of thorough data as to what the special " management " consisted of, and what sort of a ha-ha, moat, or stockade was applied to thus intercept mal-assimilation, the main excitive of the evil; for beyond the recipe of Madeira and Champagne, which might prove so much strychnine to some, it is not stated whether medical agencies were employed, or whether the palliative depended largely upon occasional fasting, heroic exercise, thermal treatment, or the avoidance of particular foods. Moreover, as this experience was chronicled over thirty years ago, it is more than likely that any efforts to trace the prophylactic would be futile. It may be re-

marked, nevertheless, that Port and Burgundy
are invariably dangerous companions, and generally hold the right bower. For is it not proverbially Port

> "That keep'st the ports of slumber open wide,
> To many a watchful night " ? —

while as regards the fermented juice of the black
Pinaud grape, the old refrain should ever be
borne in mind —

> "Burgundy rose ! Burgundy rose !
> 'T is a very bad thing at the tip of your toes ! "

Burgundy is dangerous, and the wine of the
Douro yet more so. Indeed, Petrarch never
followed the footsteps of Laura, or Herrick the
form of Anthea with greater devotion than Gout.
waits upon his favourite handmaiden, Port.

What renders Port especially harmful, apart
from the natural richness of the wine itself, is
the adventitious alcohol it always contains, with
frequently extraneous sugar and other foreign
ingredients. Sugar is also very often added to
many of the red Burgundies, to the impairment

of the colour and life of the wine, and equally to the health of the consumer. The undue proportion of Gout that has long existed in England as compared with other countries, can be traced largely to the revolution of 1688 and this addition of extraneous spirit; previous to which, and up to the date of the Methuen Treaty, the " claret " of France had been the general beverage among the wine-drinkers of Great Britain. Since 1688 the duty on French wines was raised from 1s. 4d. to 4s. 10d. per gallon, or three hundred and sixty per cent; and by the Methuen Treaty of 1703, the gates were opened wide by gouty Queen Anne for Port and its boon companion, — the produce of Portugal being received at a rate of one third less than that of France.

Since that date, down to 1831, the differential rates against French wines were never less than fifty per cent; and before the Methuen Treaty, such Port as was consumed in Great Britain was not fortified by extraneous spirit. It was in 1715 that the Portuguese first began to mingle a little brandy with the wines they sent to England, — an obnoxious custom that has largely increased up to the present time. This prohibitive tariff, a result of England's jealousy of France, became accordingly the means not only of forcing Port upon the English, but of subsequently obliging wine-consumers to drink the adulterations of an interested wine company to whom a monopoly of the Upper Douro was given in 1756. More than this, it was also the means of forcing all manner of sophisticated wines, adulterated to resemble Port, upon the consumers.

This practice of adulteration eventually spread to France. Writing in 1775, Barry states that French "claret" was largely mixed with Spanish wine at that period, and likewise complained that Port had become more heady and heating than it formerly was, requiring more time to bring it to maturity after bottling than was previously necessary.[1] From 1787 to 1810, the largest amount of Port was drunk in Great Britain ; the greatest quantity ever exported from Portugal

[1] Sir Edward Barry, *Observations on the Wines of the Ancients.*

The Proscribed Fluids

was in 1825, when 40,277 tuns, equivalent to forty thousand cases of Gout, were shipped to England. In Portugal itself, where Port is naturally drunk in considerable quantities, but is not fortified for home consumption, Gout is said to be of comparatively infrequent occurrence. The excuse made for thus vitiating the wine, is that it renders it better able to withstand the fatigue of the voyage; whereas the true and only reason for the pernicious custom is that immature wine and wine of poor years may be palmed off for old and full-bodied vintages, as also that good vintages may be sold at immaturity. Besides this adventitious alcohol, where twenty to twenty-five gallons of native brandy much above proof is frequently added to the pipe, elderberries are often freely used to impart their dye, together with sugar and *jeropiga*, — a syrup made from must, prevented from fermenting by means of spirit.

Yet as far back as 1677 Sir William Temple called attention to the fact that he had noticed no disease of that age which had increased to such an extent as Gout. His observations on wines will additionally show what kinds were then in use among the higher classes and served, in conjunction with the heavy dishes of England, to augment the malady : " But the wines used by those that feel or fear this disease, should rather be Spanish or Portugal than either French or Rhenish ; and of the French, rather the Provence or Languedoc than the Bourdeaux or Campagne; and of the Rhenish, the Rhinegaw and Bleker, of which at least it may be said that they do not so much harm as the others." [1]

The growths of Provence and Languedoc, which he recommends in preference to those of Bordeaux and Champagne, it may be noted, have always been known as heady, heavy, and fiery, in comparison with those of the Gironde and the Marne ; and were certainly ill-advised on his part for use in Gout. Sparkling Champagne in Temple's time was unknown ; and it is to be presumed, therefore, that by the word " Campagne," he has reference to the still red and white

[1] *An Essay upon the Cure of the Gout by Moxa.*

The Proscribed Fluids

products, or at most to some of the naturally
slightly effervescing products of that district, —
unless by " Campagne " some other " country "
of France was intended to be designated, which
might have been Anjou, not a few of whose
wines are also naturally slightly effervescent. It
is extremely difficult to trace or to conjecture,
however, what Rhenish wine he indicates under
the title of " Bleker," — a term unknown to the
present day, — unless he so specified some wine
of the Mosel or the Saar, or possibly of Rhenish
Bavaria.

In any event, his advice was contrary to
that of the generality of modern advisers, inasmuch as he prescribes the rich Portuguese and
full Southern wines, while he proscribes those of
Bordeaux and only admits those of the Rhine
under protest. He laid stress, likewise, on the
daily use of wine as injurious in general, argu-
ing, however fallaciously, that it having been
denied Great Britain by nature, it was never
intended for common use in that country; and
he would accordingly relegate its employment

Meditations on Gout

"for the times and occasions of feast and joy, and treating it like a mistress rather than a wife."

Heavy ales and porter are of course to be charged with their share in extending the malady; but not to the extent of Port and its adulterations. Suave, mellow, full-bodied, of a lovely colour, fragrance, and flavour, — its poison masked by unctuousness and age, — it is no wonder that this wine should have become so common a beverage in the damp climate and fogs of England, particularly at a time when the growths of the Gironde had not so generally attained the great excellence that characterises them to-day. And even now, though aware of the canker that lurks in the wine, an occasional after-dinner glass is hard to relinquish by those who may have felt its evil effects, but cling to the alluring taste of the Oporto grape. Rev. John Home, a Scottish divine and relative of David Hume, the historian and metaphysician, has told the story of Port in four lines, — the stricture having been written when a prohibitive duty on French wine was enforced in Scotland : —

The Proscribed Fluids

"Firm and erect the Caledonian stood,
Old was his mutton, and his claret good.
'Let him drink Port!' an English statesman cried;
He drank the poison, and his spirit died."[1]

It may be added that before his death in 1776, Hume attached a singular codicil to his will, relating to Port and to the author of the above epigram; Hume being fond of the wine of Portugal, and Home preferring the wine of France: "I leave to my friend, John Home of Kilduff, ten dozen of old claret at his choice, and a single bottle of that other liquor called Port. I also leave to him six dozen of Port, provided that he attests under his hand, signed John Home, that he has himself alone finished that bottle at two sittings. By this concession he will at once terminate the only two differences that ever arose between us concerning temporal matters." This was assuredly a light burden when it is considered that finishing three and four bottles at a sitting was of frequent occurrence; but historical records fail to state whether Home secured or relinquished the three score and twelve bottles of his relative's cellar.

[1] Douglas, *A Tragedy*.

Meditations on Gout

Home's invective differs from the later experience of Lord Tennyson, — like Milton a victim of Gout, — who, in his poetic fantasia to the head-waiter of the " Cock," hymns the panegyric of Port; the particular wine he sang of more than half a century ago having presumably escaped the taint of the elderberry and toxine of *jeropiga*, even though the brandy of Oporto mingled with its ruby tide : —

> " Head-waiter, honour'd by the guest
> Half-mused, or reeling-ripe,
> The pint you brought me was the best
> That ever came from pipe.
>
> . . . .
>
> " Head-waiter of the chop-house here,
> To which I most resort,
> I too must part; I hold thee dear
> For this good pint of Port."

It may be said the bard distinctly specified to the chief cup-bearer that the wine was to be perfect of its kind : —

> " But let it not be such as that
> You set before chance-comers,
> But such whose father-grape grew fat
> On Lusitanian summers."

The Proscribed Fluids

The effect was magical, as the poet exultingly testifies, — an effect that could not have been produced had the wine been otherwise than ripe and of a distinguished vintage : —

> "This earth is rich in man and maid:
>   With fair horizons bound !
> This whole wide earth of light and shade
>   Comes out a perfect round.
> High over roaring Temple-Bar,
>   And set in Heaven's third story,
> I look at all things as they are,
>   But thro' a kind of glory."

Amid the smoke and clangour of the precinct of St. Paul's, the thick crust and bees-wing sing from the poet's glass : —

> "The Muse, the jolly Muse, it is !
>   She answer'd to my call,
> She changes with that mood or this,
>   Is all-in-all to all:
> She lit the spark within my throat,
>   To make my blood run quicker,
> Used all her fiery will, and smote
>   Her life into the liquor." [1]

[1] *Will Waterproof's Lyrical Monologue.*

Meditations on Gout

Sauterne has been recommended by some writers as among the least injurious wines. In the able and interesting monograph by Dr. Frederick T. Roberts, the writer says: "Some patients are undoubtedly better if they take no stimulants whatever; others can take proper kinds in moderation with advantage. It may be laid down as a general rule that malt liquors and all stronger wines are injurious. Those wines which are most acceptable are good clarets, Hock, Mosel, Chablis, and Sauterne. Even these must only be indulged in in strict moderation. A small quantity of good dry sherry suits some patients very well. A little brandy well diluted often agrees better than any other kind of alcoholic liquor; or in some cases whisky or gin may be substituted. Whatever stimulant is selected should only be taken at meal-times, and the habit of drinking between meals is strongly to be deprecated. It is highly important that any alcoholic drink employed should be sound and of good quality."[1]

[1] *A Dictionary of Medicine*: edited by Richard Quain, M. D.

The Proscribed Fluids

It is right here — in connection with wine — that medical counsellors, with scarcely an exception, are misleading in their advice, which is invariably too general and not sufficiently specific. None of them emulate Pliny, when, referring to this all-important subject, he said, "I shall discourse of wine with gravity, approaching my topic, not as a physician, but as a judge who is to pronounce on the physical and moral health of the human race."

Instead of regarding the subject from the standpoint of the œnophilist as well as that of the therapeutist, they merely generalise, referring to the products of certain regions as more or less baneful or more or less salutary. Yet how different the various growths of a region, and even the different districts and individual growths of such districts! Take the case of Sauterne, for example, under which general term must be included not only the wines of Sauterne themselves, but those of Barsac, Bommes, Preignac, and Fargues, and often also the white wines of the Graves and Entre Deux Mers, — differing most widely in strength, dryness, bouquet, and flavour.

Furthermore, in speaking of Sauterne, it must be remembered that in all the finer wines such as Ch^au d'Yquem, Lafaurie, La Tour Blanche, Coutet, etc., there are at least four forms of the wine made from different gatherings, — the " head," " centre," " tail," and " ensemble," the latter a mixture of all three; with sometimes a still more limited, luscious first-gathering, termed the " cream." These differ very materially in the quantity of their spirituous and other constituents; notably in the amount of the saccharine element. This in turn varies immensely according to the particular year; the finer wines also being always sweeter than the ordinary growths.

To instance this great variation, one has but to recall the Ch^au d'Yquem *crême* of 1864, — a gorgeous, oily, madeira-coloured wine of surpassing softness, flavour, and sweetness, and the *tête* of the same wonderful growth of 1888, with its relatively fresh, sub-acidulous flavour. Or the deliciously unctuous, Hymettus products of Ch^au

The Proscribed Fluids

Lafaurie of 1874 and 1884, and the comparatively dry full-flavoured centre and tail wines
of 1891. It may be added that the year 1864 is
written in gold in the Sauternes district, while
that of 1888 was considered an unusually poor
vintage with white Bordeaux wines.

But let it not be inferred for a single instant
that the '88 products, or those of nearly any
year from the peerless vineyard of the Marquis
de Lur-Saluces, when bottled at the Château, are
anything less than altogether lovely! The *tête*
wine of 1888 is exquisite, as is also the *ensemble*
of 1891, and preferable, according to the writer's
taste, to the more luscious pressing of 1890.
The '61's, '64's, and '69's, alas! are past, except
as fragrant memories, — unless one may savour
them from the Marquis' *cave particulière*. Some
years are naturally more delicious and hold their
age better than others — and some are more
healthful. But one is not supposed to drink the
essence of Yquem and Lafaurie — the nectar of
the *Sémillon* and *Sauvignon* — by the magnum, or
otherwise than, on special occasions in appreciative

company, to sip a glass or two of their liquid gold at the close of the repast, with a benison to the producers, and to summon the smiling valley of the Ciron as it lies basking under the September sun.

In recommending Sauterne, therefore, it will be readily apparent that the tail wines or drier wines should alone be prescribed, or the centre wines of ordinary years, or a light white variety of the Graves, or Entre Deux Mers. A case has come under the writer's observation where Gout was manifestly developed from the daily use of a sweet Sauterne. The thin semi-acidulous wine of Vouvray is preferable to many of the Sauternes, as are also numerous white wines of Tresses, Baurech, and Sainte Croix du Mont of the Bordelais. These latter are said to be an alterative in diabetes, and of service in lessening gastralgia; they are frequently used as an aperient in Gascony, being drunk by the disciples of Nimrod on starting for the chase, — *pour tuer le ver*, according to the local expression.

Among the red wines of Bordeaux, prescribed by most physicians under the name of " clarets,"

The Proscribed Fluids

the differences in character are almost equally marked ; as, for instance, between a good ordinary St. Julien or St. Estèphe, and superior growths of the same communes, like Chᵃᵘ Léoville, Larose, and Duluc, or Chᵃᵘ Montrose, Cos d'Estournel, and Calon-Ségur. Then there are the exquisite, deep-coloured growths of Pessac, Mérignac, Léognan, and Talence of the district of the Graves, led off by Chᵃᵘ Haut-Brion, and Chᵃᵘ Haut-Bailly, among the most delicious red wines in the world, — rich, marrowy, perfumed, possessing a delightful flavour of fruits that recalls a combination of Bordeaux and Burgundy, and particularly distinguished for the quantity of iron they contain.   There are likewise the warm, generous, full-bodied products of St. Émilion and Pomerol, the former termed the red Burgundy of the Bordelais, with Chᵃᵘ Cheval Blanc as one of its best and most powerful growths.

Furthermore, not a few of the finest of the classified *crûs* of the Médoc and the Graves of the *grandes années*, on attaining a ripe age, say from fifteen to twenty years, remind one somewhat in bouquet, fulness, and flavour, of fine old Port, the spirituous and saccharine elements of course being absent. This is more noticeably the case in the growths of Margaux, some of the St. Juliens and Pauillacs, and in the Pessac first growth, Ch^au Haut-Brion.

Hock or Rhine wines are also favoured where the professional adviser sanctions the use of wine. Still, how different in qualities, ethers, and strength are the countless growths of the Rhein-gau, the Mosel, and the Saar, — the light Graacher of the Mosel with its vinous fragrance, and the strong Maximiner Grünhäuser Heeren-berger of the same district, that distils an aroma of the elder-flower. And in the upper Rhenish growths and luscious *Auslesens* of the Lower River, how dissimilar the products of the Riessling and the Traminer! — the comparatively mild Niersteiner and powerful Rüdesheimer and Rauenthaler ; and the heavy Deidesheimer Gewürz Traminer, with its pungent odour of pears, and grand golden Forster Jesuitengarten und Kirchenstück *Auslese* of the Bavarian Palatinate.

The Proscribed Fluids

Compare, too, for the sake of further illustrating the difference among red wines, Ch.ᵃᵘ Lamarque of 1884, with its bouquet and flavour somewhat identical with that of black currant jelly, and Ch.ᵃᵘ du Cartillon of 1888, of the same commune, with its entirely different, more delicate flavour resembling that of the raspberry.

It will thus be manifest at a glance how divergent are different growths of a given class of wines, as well as these same growths of different years; how varied their ethers, the amount of alcohol, acids, salts, tannin, and other ingredients they contain; how some may act as powerful stimulants, others as diuretics, and still others as soothing corroborants. Some are dry, others slightly sweet, or extremely saccharine; some are sprightly, acting favourably upon the digestion; some are soft, rich, and marrowy; while all vary to a greater or lesser degree in their special bouquets and flavours. Young wines, in addition, always differ from old wines in that many of their constituent properties are not yet precipitated, but still retained in the fluid; and often the former, from their greater briskness, agree better with some than the older, softer kinds. This applies only to the more ordinary varieties; the finer sorts should either be left alone or only drunk at maturity. "The thinnest, whitest, smallest Wine is best, not thick nor strong; and so of Beer the middling is the fittest," quoth Master Robert Burton, in his cure for melancholy.

Little, if any, attention has been given by medical writers to the effects of white Burgundies; the term "Burgundy" usually being understood to mean a red wine of marked alcoholic potency, highly charged with uric toxine, and a near relative of Port. It is questionable, however, whether some of the white growths of the Côte d'Or are not fully as admissible as those of the Rheingau — due regard being paid to the individual with whom white wines may or may not agree. Not a few of the white growths of Burgundy are less acid than those of the Rhine district, and often possess more unctuousness, without being sweet, and with no more or little more alcoholic force. There are very heady white Burgundies, as there

are very fiery Rhine wines; and among the white
growths of the Côte d'Or there exist a great
variety — from the variable *ordinaire*, and dry
and potent Pouilly, with its flinty taste, or the
well-known Chablis, to the suave, nutty Meur-
sault and priceless Montrachet. It remains for
the analyst and physiologist to say whether the
elements the Chaudenay grape has extracted
from the soil are more or less salutary than those
of its rival, the Riessling.

As between white wines and red wines, the
patient himself will be able to decide to the best
advantage; the former acting adversely with
some upon the nervous system, as well as provoking acidity; the latter proving astringent,
heating, or binding, to others. White wines are
usually most stimulating and most rapidly absorbed; red wines most nutritive and blood-pro-
ducing. The matter of "nerves" would not
appear to enter into the case in Germany, where
the principal wines drunk are the products of the
Rhine, and where nervousness is almost an unknown quantity; whereas with the more impres-

sionable French, Bordeaux or some species of red wine is the form most generally consumed.

The consideration, however, of the hygienic qualities of red versus white wines for certain conditions or temperaments is a very old one. Leaving the ancients out of the question, as long ago as the middle of the sixteenth century, when Sack, Canary, Malmsey, Muscadel, Rhenish, Rochelle (or the wines of the provinces of Poitou and Saintonge), Guienne, and Gascony were drunk in Great Britain, — Dean William Turner called attention to the dissimilar effects of white and red species, with reference, if not to Gout, at least to a somewhat kindred kidney disorder, gravel. "Both French, Clared, and Gascony wines are not thin and subtle," he declares, "but strong, thick, and hot." His comments on "claret," by which presumably he implies a red wine from Guienne no less than Gascony, would indicate, as is familiar to many, that the red wines of the Bordelais at that period were of an entirely different quality and made from different grapes than they are now. It is known that the growths of the Dordogne, adjoining that of the Gironde, both of which provinces are in the department of Guienne, together with the products of Tarn, and also those of Macau, Margaux, Blaye, Bourg, and other communes of the Médoc proper, were largely consumed in England in olden days, when the demand was for robust, " strong, sharp, and full-flavoured " wines. So that the strictures of the author relative to "claret" become perfectly intelligible, and apply with equal force at present to many kinds of wine, though not to the Médoc growths. " Both French, Clared, and Gascony Clared wines," he continues, "are of grosser and thicker substance, and hotter of complexion than white Rhenish wine and white French wines be of : therefore they breed the stone more than white Rhenish and white French wines do." [1]

All the white wines of the Bordelais and also of the Rhine, whatever the varieties of grapes of which they were formerly composed, we know were pressed from a single gathering, and not

---

[1] *Notes on Wines in England ; A New Book on the Nature and Properties of Wines, etc.* (1568).

Meditations on Gout

from different gatherings or grain by grain, as is now the case in the Sauternes district and as also prevails extensively in the finer growths of the Rheingau and Rhenish Bavaria.

From what has been observed respecting different kinds of wine, it may readily be conceived that a mistake in the choice of growths may be the means of involving a whole train of arthritic disasters. For while water has been pronounced dangerous, wine is still less to be trifled with. *Remarquez qu'une seule erreur sème de la graine d'erreur*, says Chevreul, — a precept that applies with striking relevancy to Gout. If a single bottle of wine may sometimes summon the enemy, how much more may a binful of a certain *crû*, where it disagrees with a particular subject, invite a chronic dyscrasia that may lead to chalkstones, or end in smiting the heart with fatal results!

How all-important, then, that one should only drink such species and varieties as are best suited to his peculiar constitution, condition, and temperament; or drink a white or a red wine according as it assimilates best with the kinds of food

The Proscribed Fluids

to be partaken of! Fancy a person who is re-
stricted by his physician to " claret," washing
down his Blue-Points with a sour St. Julien to
set up an acetous fermentation; or another, who
is confined to sherry, deluging a capon with
Amontillado! " Idiosyncrasy is as apt to be as
marked in respect to wine as in respect to articles
of diet, and should be taken into account," observes Ewart. " The qualities we should look
for in a wine for habitual use," he adds, " are a
moderate percentage of alcohol and of ethers;
the least possible degree of acidity; freedom
from unfermented sugar as far as this is consist-
ent with a natural unadulterated condition; freedom from tannin; genuineness as to vintage, or
at least, as to derivation, mixed wines being most
likely to do harm; and, lastly, mature age.
The difficulty in securing these essentials is perhaps greater now than at any previous period,
and adds to the strength of the general objection
to wines in Gout." [1]

[1] Dr. William Ewart, *Gout and Goutiness and their
Treatment.*

Meditations on Gout

While Champagne is invariably invested with a red flag of danger, as Port is always labelled, "Look out for the cars!" — it may well be questioned if the charge against it be not much too sweeping, and whether, if moderately partaken of in a rather dry form and of irreproachable quality, it does not act as a tonic and digester. Still, like many other things, this will depend upon the individual, — human digestion being as varied in its complexion as the human physiognomy. Among medical authorities who have written upon the subject at length, Granville is virtually the only exception in recommending the use of Champagne in Gout.[1] This wine was also favoured in the past century by Sir Edward Barry, Fellow of the Royal College of Physicians.[2]

As bad cookery is responsible for much indigestion, and as wine varies so greatly in its component parts and the effects of its varieties upon

[1] Dr. J. Mortimer Granville, *Notes and Conjectures on Gout.*

[2] *Observations on the Wines of the Ancients.*

The Proscribed Fluids

various persons, may not the obstinacy of the malady be largely dependent, accordingly, upon the excellence or the demerits of the cuisine and the wine-cellar? Again, as diversity in foods is a most important dietetic consideration, does it not follow, *pari passu*, that a diversity of wines is of equal consequence? Instead of being hedged in with one kind, therefore, which soon palls upon the taste, may not an ampler vinous pasturage be chosen, and a variety, within certain bounds, be vastly more desirable?

It has already been observed that certain fruits disagree with certain individuals. The delicious strawberry, in particular, is a violent poison to many, having frequently proved an excitant in developing an attack of Gout; and despite Dr. Boteler's eulogy, it is known to be prolific of violent gastralgia, painful urticaria, and intense stomatitis. Others experience disastrous effects from eating raspberries, red and black currants, apples, quinces, oranges, bananas, grape-fruit, and various other fruits, both native and tropical.

How, then, can a physician prescribe wine in-

telligently, which invariably resembles or suggests some kind of fruit, without being not only
familiar with the constitution of his patient,
and his physical likes and dislikes, but also without being a wine-drinker himself, and intimately
acquainted with the varieties of wines? No
doubt, also, many of those who are subject to
Gout are equally ignorant in this respect; and
some particular growth or growths, or some
particular species that they are in the habit of
drinking, counts for an important cause of their
stomachic derangement so far as wines are concerned.

For why should not the elemental parts contained in wine be as important a factor as those
contained in mineral waters and natural springs,
which differ so greatly in their effects? But with
the doctors, as in *As You Like It*, wine invariably " comes out of a narrow-mouthed bottle;
either too much at once, or none at all." Clearly,
the doctors are at fault; and wine may after all
be a good familiar creature, and the sun's best
use be " to warm the grape." As in angling,

The Proscribed Fluids

"all winds are hurtful if too hard they blow," and the worst of winds is an east wind; so with wine, all kinds may be harmful if partaken of too generously, and of these Port and Burgundy are the most detrimental.

As wine, with its engaging perfume and exhilarating flavour, is so efficacious in many forms of sickness; as it proves so cheering to the senses and provocative of good-fellowship when partaken of in moderation; as, moreover, the vine grows, and thrives, and ripens its ruby, roseate, and golden fruit on arid soils where no other useful plants could find a sustenance, — would it not seem a natural consequent that its expressed juices were pre-eminently designed by Nature for the health and solace of mankind? And differing so widely as constitutions do, may not a potent cause of the disease under consideration be the use of certain forms that are inimical to the individual, rather than to the mere use of wine *per se?*

A person who is subject to Gout, therefore, should exercise the greatest care in the choice of such wines as meet his particular requirements; and having once found such growths, he should religiously abstain from the ordinary wines of commerce, however alluring the labels and golden the capsules. A conscientious wine-merchant, accordingly, who has the reputation of vineyards of his own at stake, a merchant who is thoroughly familiar with the wines of his district, and who may be absolutely relied upon to send samples not only true to name, but of a *mise irréprochable* so far as their bottling is concerned, becomes the greatest essentiality in a cure of Gout by the means of wine. His price is above rubies, and his remedy needs no bush. To the majority of wine-drinkers, however, this great desideratum exists solely as an unknown quantity. And when one further considers the marvellous versatility of the French *barrique*, under the necromancy of numerous middlemen, to discharge "St. Julien," "Pontet-Canet," and "Ch^au Larose" by a mere turn of the spigot, the difficulty of procuring a pure wine, true to name, becomes the more readily apparent. It may be asserted

The Proscribed Fluids

within bounds that the average annual production of the Pauillac vineyard of Pontet-Canet, amounting to one hundred and eighty tuns, would not suffice for a tenth part of the wine which is consumed under that name alone.

With relation to the cure of Gout through the use of wine, the following dialogue which took place in the writer's presence, is presented verbatim for the benefit of the afflicted. A short time since two distinguished prelates, who are fond of the pleasures of the table and who are both occasionally troubled with arthritic complaints, met on the street after a somewhat extended absence.

"*Ah! bon jour, Monsignor,*" observed the one; "I am delighted above measure. Have you been abroad again and just returned?"

"*Mais non, mon cher Révérend,*" was the reply; "it has been too hot this summer for travelling, and now it is too damp in Europe. You know we must be careful and nurse our rheumatism."

"Surely! and in order the better to correct it,

Meditations on Gout

we cannot be too guarded in drinking any but the very best wine."

"*Mais oui !*" replied Monsignor, with emphasis; "*et jamais laisser une goutte dans son verre.*"

The *mot* of the eminent prelate and the advice of his right-reverend confrère are certainly worthy of embalming; the antidote and prescription being much more agreeable than colchicum; though good wine — "*l'honnête verre où rit un peu d'oubli divin*" — is far less readily procured. Let it not be understood, however, that this ecclesiastical counsel was intended to apply to wine in general. For while both of the distinguished divines attribute their usual well-being to its moderate employment, their vinous indulgence consists principally in the delicate juices of the Cabernet, Merlot, and Malbec of the Médoc, of well-succeeded years, to the almost entire exclusion of the fierier growths of the Côte d'Or and the South, — a case of Timothy's "a little wine for thy stomach's sake," rather than Rabelais's "*fontaine caballine.*"

The Proscribed Fluids

In a similar vein of advice to the ecclesiastical counsel recorded, are the lines of Maistre Jean Le Houx : —

> *" La goutte ung drolle n' affronte,*
> *Qui boit sans songier au compte :*
> *Auares en sont saiʒis,*
> *Qui ont les escus moiʒis."*

> Gout attacks not merry sot
> Cost of drink who counteth not;
> Misers are of gout diseased,
> Who have crowns by mildew seized.

One will also recall the dialogue between the Old Man and the Physician, in the inimitable *Chansons du Vaux de Vire*, where good wine is likewise prescribed as a cure : —

. . . . . .

LE VIEILLARD.

> *La goutte aux joinctures des os*
> *Me tient alors que le temps change,*
> *Si bien que j'en pers le ʒepoʒ.*

LE MÉDECIN.

> *De decoction de vendange*
> *Recipe, trois voltes & plus :*
> *Ne songe tant en tes escus.*

165

Meditations on Gout

LE VIEILLARD.

Tous vos receptes sont de vin,
Le vin, est ce choʒe si bonne ?
Sans lui ne serieʒ médecin !

LE MÉDECIN.

À tous ceulx-là le vin j'ordonne,
Qui en humeur me sont égaulx,
Car le vin garit tous mes maulx.

OLD MAN.

In change of weather gout doth keep
   The joints of all my bones in pain,
So that at night I cannot sleep.

PHYSICIAN.

   Recipe : — Three times o'er again,
And more, decoction of the vine;
Don't heed so much those crowns of thine.

OLD MAN.

Your Recipes are always wine.
   Is wine so very good a thing?
Without it, fails your medecine !

PHYSICIAN.

I 'm always safe in ordering
Those of my humour such a dose;
For wine alone cures all my woes.

The Proscribed Fluids

Indeed, floating with the jolly Norman bard upon the roseate tide of the *Vaux de Vire*, it is difficult not to believe that alone by the generous use of wine may one expect to avoid Gout, but equally the countless petty miseries of life which charge upon one on every side, — that for all mundane ailments and vexations, the fermented juice of the grape is the sole and supreme nepenthe. Like the olden handwriting upon the wall, his *morale* ever stands out in bold italic type: —

> *Auec repos, auec contentement*
> *Vsons des biens que le Ciel nous enuoye ;*
> *Il ne faut pas, faute d'vn peu de ioye,*
> *Le bec en l'eau, nos jours precipiter.*

> In rest and sweet contentment let us take
> The blessings Heav'n deigns lovingly to send ;
> And not for lack of what some joy can lend,
> By water-drinking, death anticipate.[1]

[1] James Patrick Muirhead's translation.

THE QUANDARY

THE QUANDARY

The grief thereof him wondrous sore diseas'd,
Ne might his rankling pain with patience be appeas'd.

SPENSER.

T will be seen that no thera-
peutist as yet, in this great
age of progress, has thrown
an X-ray on the prevention
and cure of the malady. According to general medical
consension, it is as impossible to eradicate it, as
it is to cultivate the *Edelweiss* or the *Maenner-
treu*. It virtually remains where it was in
Sydenham's day, with colchicum and abstinence
as its chief specifics, which are within the means
of every one to prescribe.

It is obdurate and implacable. Once the
precedent formed by the stomach of allowing
alcoholic fluids and gravies to rush into the
feet ; once the enemy having been permitted to

obtain a foothold — it is next to impossible to rout him effectually, whatever the means of defence adopted. He may be starved out possibly, at the expense of the general health; but all the halberds, hauberks, and arblasts of the physicians are powerless to banish him permanently. And as the dinner is the true promoter, abettor, and accomplice of the malady, it would seem that it is only by cutting off this meal entirely that one may hope to overcome the foe.

A weathercock as well as a wolf, the disease is not only extremely protean throughout its manifold forms, but in its erratic moods of a single form. The slightest pretext may sometimes induce its recurrence; as, on the contrary, more particularly in the acute form, one may escape an attack for a long period, though the enemy be unduly and even persistently provoked.

" There is no disease," observes John Mason Good, who was a sufferer himself, " to which the human frame is subject, that has led to such a variety of opinions, many of them directly contradictory to each other; and, I may add, there

The Quandary

is no disease concerning the nature and treatment of which physicians are so little agreed ; so that to this moment it constitutes perhaps the widest field for empiricism, and the hottest for warfare of any that lie within the domain of medical science,"[1] — an echo of Cullen's phrase: "The gout, not only as it occurs in different persons, but even as it occurs in the same person at different times, is a disease of such various appearance that it is difficult to render the history of it complete and exact, or to give a character of it that will universally apply."[2] "We feel convinced," remarks Trousseau, "notwithstanding the pretensions of modern medicine, that we have made no advance since the time of Sydenham in our knowledge in the treatment, phenomena, and special nature of gout."[3]

In view of these declarations by the *Magi* themselves, how may the patient be guided ? To abide by the counsels of numerous advisers is a

[1] *The Study of Medicine.*
[2] *First Lines of the Practice of Physic.*
[3] *Lectures on Clinical Medicine.*

physical impossibility. To carry out that of any given one may even be attended with fatal results, as Trousseau himself has recounted in the case of a patient whom he had in charge during his early practice.

At the best, the victim will experience a sorry time. No longer may his waistcoat wear the enseigne of Rabelais, *Fay ce que voudras*, but rather bear the burden of Lucretius, *Surgit amari aliquid*, as he dons the sackcloth of vegetarianism or submits to the martyrdom of hydropathy. Good-cheer may no longer be his; each dish must forever be weighed in the balance. There may be no more *sauce Tartare,* no *vol au vents,* no lobster *à la* Newburgh, no *œufs Commadore* — no Volnay, no Bass, no *Münchner!* He must perforce be metred, and at the table have water flow as freely as Champagne. For the mantling beads of the Marne, he must be content with the riotous gurgle of Apollinaris, or drown his sorrows in a geyser. Arise he must betimes, and seek communion with the dawn. In place of courting the whims of his palate, he must cater to

The Quandary

the vagaries of his stomach. He must eschew society, and make friends with his porridge. Hear the dismal chorus of his monitors!

Gouty patients should be absolutely forbidden to go to dinners even if they promise to be very moderate (Niemeyer); salmon, pork, veal, and salads are to be avoided (Aitken); it is essential to be very sober, and not to eat food difficult of digestion (Trousseau); his beverage should be cool and unstimulant (Good); acid articles should be forbidden (Strümpell); to prevent overloading the stomach, the number of meals should be limited (Senator); beer and ale in any form are to be avoided (Mendelson); we must strictly regulate the hours of his meals (Sydenham); pastry of all kinds should be interdicted (Roberts); asparagus is to be avoided or used with great moderation; tomatoes, rhubarb, and sorrel are exceedingly acid, and usually disagree (Ewart).

Nor is this sufficient; all looks yellow to their jaundic'd eye.

A captain's biscuit or two, thoroughly soaked in milk and water, is the best bread food (Chambers) ; Champagne, sherries, Burgundy, Madeira, the different Rhine and Mosel wines should be carefully avoided (Hare) ; those wines which are most acceptable are good clarets, hock, Mosel, Chablis, and Sauterne (Roberts); extreme moderation should be observed when saccharine fruits are eaten (Garrod); spirits have a tendency to cause both fatty and fibrous degeneration, while a single glass of port wine will often produce painful twinges, and a similar effect is not infrequently noticed from hock, Champagne also often exciting an attack in gouty persons (Morris); all culinary delicacies should be absolutely forbidden (Senator).

Still the chorus continues — unyieldingly, determinedly, prohibitively, contradictorily :

A casual glass or two of Champagne may suffice to bring the enemy suddenly upon one (Watson) ; some are inclined to look upon the albuminoids as most injurious, while others consider the carbo-hydrates equally as bad (Hare) ; dry sherry and the light wines, as claret, Burgundy, hock, Champagne, etc., may be drunk, certainly in moderation, although any kind of

The Quandary

wine appears capable of sometimes acting as the exciting cause of a paroxysm (Pavy); spirits and the drier wines are the best suited to gouty persons, wines having much less tendency than spirits to damage the liver, and much less tendency than malt-liquors to bring on gout (Budd); gin is to be preferred from its diuretic tendency (Flint); there is no such thing as a temperate use of spirits (Alden); dried apples, pears, and prunes form a pleasant desert for the gouty (Mendelson); this disease seldom attacks eunuchs (Cullen).

Avoid foods that please and drink drinks that displease! they cry in concert, if not in unison, — and the scourge of Gout will wield a softer thong; by thus abstaining you may not hope to avert the lash, it is true, but the number of the strokes may be lessened. It is but the oft repeated cry, most tersely expressed by Jacques Tahureau in his poem, *De La Vanité des Hommes:*

"Tout ce que l'homme fait, tout ce que l'homme pense
    En ce bas monde ici,
N'est rien qu'un vent legier, qu'une vaine espérance
    Plaine d'un vain souci.

Meditations on Gout

"L'homme mortel n'est rien qu'une simple fumée
    Qui passe tout soudain;
Ce n'est rien qu'une poudre a tous vens promenée
    Que de ce cors humain."

[All that man does, all that man thinks
    In this world here below,
Is but the breath of a breeze, a hope unattain'd,
    Full of care and of woe.

For man is scarce more than a shifting shade,
    To come and to pass;
And nought but a powder and toy of the wind,
    Is his body, alas!]

Verily, in so much wisdom there is much grief; and manifestly he who would increase his knowledge but increaseth his sorrow. In the name of the lovely goddess Hygeia, and in the face of so many prescriptions and proscriptions, what is the poor sufferer to do to avoid not only acute Gout, but suppressed, cerebral, asthenic, anomalous, gastro-enteric, cardiac, diaphragmatic, visceral, chalky, metastatic, extra-articular, and the "flying" form — except to flee from the Gradgrinds and resign himself to his fate?

The great desideratum — a sure alterative, cor-

The Quandary

rective, or an astomotic that will anticipate and foil the foe—remains hopelessly undiscovered. Where the vaunted pharmacopœia of the menders of disease — the countless herbs, barks, and products of the vegetable and mineral kingdoms that exist for the healing of the nations? And while doctors continue to disagree, who shall decide?

It has been shown that besides many other organs, the spleen is possibly connected in some occult way with the diathesis of the disorder, and has its part to play in the dyscrasia. Yet how often do we hear of a physician alluding to this mysterious functionary; or, in the case of Gout, attempting to force it to maintain the peace of the internal household? To all but Professor Senator its exact rôle would appear to be utterly unknown. How many of the moderns are even aware that they possess a spleen? The ancients were wiser, and rightly held it to be the seat of melancholy and anger. What doctor withal has devoted so much as an instant's thought to the comforts that might be afforded by so simple a

Meditations on Gout

support and means of defence as an *Alpenstock* within constant reach of the patient ? [1] And who beyond Fothergill has ever noted that the east wind finds out the liver, albeit it lies intrenched beneath the diaphragm and is carefully guarded by the abdominal walls? [2] "The east wind comes with sickness on its wings," saith the author of *A Club of One,* " and rejoiceth only the doctor and the sexton." Mist and fog that shroud the landscape, yet bring near-by objects into more than usual relief, are likewise known to accentuate disturbances of the system. The weather, therefore, may be responsible for much more in the ætiology of disease than it has been credited with by medical writers who have attempted to interpret the phenomena of disease. And of all the phases and mutations of the weather-vane, the east wind is most irritating to arthritic affections; and, accordingly, may be a potent though as yet unacknowledged cause of Gout.

[1] Gouty patients generally acquire a morose, susceptible, and irascible temper, formerly foreign to them. — TROUSSEAU.

[2] Dr. J. Milner Fothergill, *Indigestion and Biliousness.*

The Quandary

Neither, to speak in all seriousness, have medical advisers, with scarcely an exception, in their treatment of the subject, referred to one of the great promoters of the malady, inasmuch as it constitutes one of the most frequent sources of indigestion, — rapid eating, and eating between meals, or drinking alcoholic beverages between meals. Writers are equally silent regarding the use of tobacco. Whether this may prove an excitant in a reflex way to those predisposed, through its effects upon the nervous system, as well as upon the gastric functions, is a question worthy of consideration, the more so as a smoker invariably smokes to his full capacity. The same may be said respecting some other features of dietetics, notably the failure of physicians to insist upon their patients who may be addicted to the use of stimulants, to make a point of always drinking an equal quantity of water at their meals.

Sydenham and Cullen are almost alone in emphasising constipation as, if not a direct, at any rate an indirect cause of Gout in numerous instances. Insufficient stress, likewise, is laid upon change of air and scene, which means equally a change of diet, for those who may be predisposed or who have acquired the malady. Undoubtedly the advantages of periodical abstention and dieting, constitute one of the best prophylactics. Moreover, to thoroughly enjoy a thing, one needs to experience occasional denial. Few are aware of the voluptuousness of asceticism practised at intervals, in the renewed zest it gives to the palate, and the rest it imparts to a jaded digestion. Thus the Lenten abnegation enjoined by the Catholic religions, in place of a penance becomes a stomachic ; and the Friday fast of the Roman Catholic church a most excellent sanitary measure.

Why attempt to pamper to appetite until appetite rebels, or try to combat the stomach when the stomach cries for rest ? There invariably comes a time when we all must say, *Bonjour lunettes ! adieu fillettes !* What signifies a savoury *entrée* or an hour of gustatory delight, compared with the penalties they exact ? And, after

The Quandary

all, is it not mainly the first step in renunciation
which costs? "Begin a reformation, and custom
will make it easy," saith Elia. And quoth wise
Montaigne, "All meanes that may bring us unto
health cannot be esteemed of men either sharpe
or deare." Once the patient has practised ab-
stemiousness for a short period, he will find his
path a flowery one, freed to a large extent from
the tares of indigestion. The over-taxed stomach
will regain its tone, the liver its sprightliness.
Plethora will gradually diminish, the senses become sharpened, and a state of well-being ensue
that will doubly recompense him for his forbear-
ance, and place him in position to enjoy the dinners that the future holds in store. "All is habit,
even virtue itself," Metastasio has declared ; and
appetite and habit notoriously grow upon that by
which they are nourished. Again, it would be
well for all to ponder a wise sentence of Temple's :
"It is certain that pleasures depend upon the
temper of the body; and that to enjoy them a
man must be well himself, as the vessel must be
sound to have your wine sweet. Whoever will

eat well must have a stomach; who will relish the pleasure of drinks must have his mouth in taste; who will enjoy a beautiful woman must be in vigour himself." [1]

These reflections necessarily lead to the consideration of a matter of still greater moment — the neglect in the schools and colleges and seats of learning of sufficiently recognising and inculcating hygiene, through lack of which one does not learn until too late the penalties attached to the violation of its statutes or the consequences entailed by an insufficient knowledge of the laws of health. Then, when disease attacks and ills assail, one realises how easy the preventive would have been if applied in time.

While it will be sufficiently apparent from the foregoing remarks, which refer to the treatment of the malady, that no detailed formula can be laid down to cover each separate instance, but that each in a certain measure calls for a different mode of procedure, still, the following observations will be applicable to the majority of cases :—

[1] On Health and Long Life.

The Quandary

First of all, anything that tends to promote general health will prove of immediate benefit, — such as regular hours; moderation in drinking; plain though nourishing food; the avoidance of rich, sweet, and heavy wines, and where wine is drunk the use for the most part of a sound Bordeaux, a light white Graves or Entre Deux Mers, or a *Tischwein* of the Rheingau or Mosel; the abstention from malt liquors, notably Porter and heavy ales; the abstemious use of sweets and acids; abundance of open air and exercise; and sufficient change of air and scene. To these may be added the use of lithia or potash, and mild laxatives if required, or such tonics, aperients, or diuretics as one's medical adviser may prescribe; the avoidance of rapid eating, worry, and undue excitement; the employment of cool baths or the Turkish bath; and a thorough use of the flesh-brush or crash-towel twice a day.

Or, to place the matter in another form — where one has been accustomed to a full and liberal dietary, it should be reduced; where it has been illiberal, it should be enriched. In the one case the steam must be shut off ; in the other, turned on. In any event, it is unadvisable to starve or to feast. Where mind or body has been overtaxed, it should be soothed; where sedentary habits have prevailed, regular exercise must ever be brought to bear, whilst one's motto must be elimination, elimination, elimination! through the kidneys, through the bowels, through the skin. If the kidneys are blocked, or the bowels sluggish, the remaining emunctory is the skin ; and this has its influence, and should be rigorously spurred into action.

It may be said that wine in Gout is one of those things it is hard to get along with, and hard to get along without. To proscribe it, to a person who has long been accustomed to it, is to tamper with his digestion and general health; to prescribe it as a tonic or digestive, as vaguely prescribed by the doctors, is to present a vulnerable point to the enemy. The patient who is naturally subject to the malady, thus stands between two fires — the torch of dyspepsia and the touchwood of arthriticism, with little hope of

The Quandary

escaping the flames in either case. But with reference to wine, it may be observed that there are wines and wine; and he who turns these pages must be artless indeed who cannot read sufficiently between the lines to choose a sort that will aid him in his cure, and bear out the exegesis of the persuasive Advocate of Vire : —

> *Se treuuent trois lettres en Vin,*
> *Qui font Vigueur, Ioie, Nourriture,*
> *Et dénotent bien sa nature,*
> *Comme dict fort bien mon voisin.*

> Three letters which in VIN are found
> Mean *Vigour, Joy,* and *Nutriment :*
> My neighbour well says, thus are meant
> Three gifts that in good wine abound.

It is from good wine alone, of course, that any alleviation may be expected. Wine in itself is a dangerous expedient; and it cannot be reiterated too often that *it is only by employing the exact kind,* best suited to the requirements of the particular individual and stage of the malady, that one may hope to outflank and elude the foe.

THE INDUCTION

THE INDUCTION

Cogimur a suetis animum suspendere rebus :
Atque ut vivamus, vivere desinimus.

Pseudo-Gallus.

From things erst us'd we must suspend our minde,
We leave to live that we may live by kinde.

T may finally be observed that Gout is but a comparatively minor infliction among the countless physical ailments which in various guises assail the human race, — that the man or woman who is permanently exempt from any constitutional disorder, be it inherited or acquired, is a far greater anomaly than exists in any disease itself. Eucrasy, or absolute soundness of health in the human species, is as rare as the unicorn in the animal kingdom: for if man, as he rounds out his half century of the brief span allotted him, be besieged by no organic evils, it is

a thousand to one that he is harrowed by some infirmity of the mind or senses. For hath it not been decreed that every man shall bear his own burden, and he that is born of a woman is of few days and full of trouble? Even the chronic sufferer, if he be afflicted by no other malady and hampered by no impairment of the sensory functions, has much to be thankful for. If he be deprived of the pleasures of the table to a great degree, he may yet contemplate a monk of Tambourini holding up his glass of wine upon the canvas, or peruse the *Almanach des Gourmands* and *The Physiology of Taste*, with no dread of arthritic pains to follow. With smiling landscapes upon his walls and Oriental rugs upon his floors, he may still revel in colours as rich as those the vat reveals; and in the flowers of his garden find bouquets to rival those of the best succeeded Haut-Brion and Montrachet. His cigar and his brier will have lost none of their fragrance and consolation, while possibly even in water he will be enabled to discover virtues not dreamed of in his erstwhile philosophy. From

the table, he can turn with renewed appreciation
to the tomes of the moralists, and find an added
charm in the musings of Pascal and Montaigne.
Delights innumerable may still be his — the
world has not grown old : —

" The boon thou hast not had,
'T is a slight, trivial thing to make thee sad,
When with the sunshine and the storm God's glorious
world is glad.

.   .   .   .

" The word is not yet said
Of ultimate ending, we are quick, not dead,
Though the dim years withhold from us one frail joy
coveted.

" Our life is all too brief,
The world too wide, too wonderful for grief,
Too crowded with the loveliness of bird and bud and leaf.

" So though we said good-bye
With bitter futile tears, my dream and I —
Each slender blade of wayside grass is clothed with
majesty." [1]

Perchance the most philosophical way for the
sufferer is to take up a treatise of medicine, and

[1] A Morning Walk, *Cornhill Magazine.*

perusing it attentively, note the innumerable ills that flesh is heir to which are infinitely worse than his own. And while he ponders over life's uncertainties and recognises that mankind was created to suffer and endure, as well as to rejoice and enjoy, if he be a minute philosopher he may conclude his reflections with this corollary, as, were he not afflicted with Gout, he might top off his dinner with a glass of Port,— in one form or another, sooner or later, one must pay the penalty of living; and what can a man live long enough to know except that he is born to die ?

INDEX

INDEX

Index

Index

Index

Index

Index

Index

Index

Index

Index

Index

Index

www.ingramcontent.com/pod-product-compliance
Lightning Source LLC
Chambersburg PA
CBHW030115030726
47498CB00007B/2398